MASTERING
MEDIOCRITY

JIM & MARGEE,

YOUR POSITIVE INFLUENCE HAS
TRANSCENDED MULTIPLE GENERATIONS
OF MY FAMILY. WE ARE FOREVER
GRATEFUL.

WITH LOVE & RESPECT!

TODD & LISA

MASTERING MEDIOCRITY

BECOME THE BEST VERSION OF YOU

TODD FLOWERS

XULON PRESS

Xulon Press
2301 Lucien Way #415
Maitland, FL 32751
407.339.4217
www.xulonpress.com

© 2020 by Todd Flowers

Unless otherwise indicated, Scripture quotations taken from the King James Version (KJV) –*public domain*.

Printed in the United States of America

Paperback ISBN-13: 978-1-6322-1171-2
Ebook ISBN-13: 978-1-6322-1172-9

DEDICATION

I AM DEDICATING THIS BOOK TO THE WOMAN WHO HAS never left my side through the best of times and our share of the challenging times. We have the family we enjoy today because of your tireless commitment to always being the example to everyone around you. I love you with all my heart. Thank you for continuing to inspire me to become a better man. Lisa Flowers, you are my angel.

FOREWORD

OVER THE COURSE OF MY LIFE I HAVE BEEN BLESSED TO meet, and in some cases, develop a long-term personal relationship with a number of men and women who have achieved great success in their lives. Many are considered to be leaders in the areas of business, education, politics, athletics, law enforcement, entertainment, and spiritual matters.

All of these people have accomplished great success in their chosen field, and some have made a positive difference in the lives of untold numbers of people. From them, I have learned what to do, and perhaps more importantly, what not to do to achieve success in my own personal and business life. However, apart from my own family, my greatest reward has been helping and observing individuals and couples achieve great success in both their personal and professional lives.

Todd Flowers is one of a handful of people I've known over the years who has consistently demonstrated personal growth, a teachable spirit, and success in virtually every area of his life. Honesty, integrity and transparency are at the core of who he has become as he has interacted with others and built his incredible business. At the same time, he and his lovely wife Lisa have raised a beautiful family which now includes several young grandchildren. This balance of super success in business as well as prioritizing family is obviously rare, worth knowing about, and emulating.

As you read Todd's powerful story of overcoming tremendous challenges as a young person and going through the fire of discovering his unlimited potential, you will perhaps be inspired to do more with your own life. At the center of his success is an unwavering application of his personal priorities, which are:

1. God
2. Family
3. Country
4. Others

Being consistent and persistent in applying these priorities along with an incredible work ethic are at the core of his success. His ultimate message in this book is, "If I can do it, you can do it. You just have to want it badly enough."

There are many people who are thankful to Todd Flowers for his unwavering commitment to excellence and success, as he has provided a roadmap and opportunity for others to reach their dreams and goals as well. I am particularly thankful that he took the time to share his personal struggles and successes with those of us still hungry enough to benefit from them.

Jim Floor
International Entrepreneur

INTRODUCTION

A COUPLE YEARS AGO I ATTENDED A BUSINESS FORUM. We had a moderator come in to share some new ideas. Little did I know that in the next hour the moderator would inspire me to do something I never thought I would do.

He told us to pretend we had just died and to write a message to our kids for them to read and remember us by. What would I say? What would I want them to know about me? It was a very heavy topic to digest in twenty minutes. The small group I was in sat very still, quietly writing. Time passed incredibly fast.

The second part of the exercise was to read what you wrote to the other people sitting at your table. I happened to be at a table comprised entirely of men. As they read their letters, they struggled to get the words out.

Many had tears streaming down their faces. It was no different for me. I'm a "courtesy crier." I read what I wrote while thinking of things I wish I could've thought of before. My heart was so full of love for my family and I was so grateful for their blessing in my life. The third and final part of the exercise was to share our take-a-ways.

I told my table mates that I had decided to take this endeavor further. I would carry a notepad with me so I could journal my memories, thoughts and ideas for my family to one day read after

I die. I was caught up in the emotion of the moment, but I meant what I said.

I was so convicted that two years passed, and I hadn't written down a single thing. Then, inspiration found me. I experienced some health issues that caused me to reflect on my life. I decided to take action on ideas I had been procrastinating on.

I shared my new idea with my wife Lisa and daughter Melissa. I thought rather than journal random thoughts, why not write my story in the form of a book? Melissa said it could be a manifesto for my grandchildren and great grandchildren to read one day.

I sat on the idea until February 2020 when the coronavirus changed how we would live for the next few months. Most of my business would shelter in place when every casino in the country shut their doors.

To keep our team ready to attack when the virus would end, we developed a program that included personal and professional growth. I also encouraged our team to start something for themselves that they have been putting off.

I thought to myself that I had better practice what I was preaching, so what the heck, I started writing this book. Very few people knew (until now!) about this crazy idea, but the process was truly life changing. Mediocre, or average effort produces a mediocre lifestyle. In my own life I was not willing to settle for mediocrity when I knew I had the ability to be better than average. I am confident that you can take away some proven strategies from this book that can change your life as well.

PROLOGUE

I'M STANDING ON THE SIXTEENTH FLOOR OF A VERY upscale building in Beverly Hills peering through giant plate glass windows overlooking the Los Angeles Country Club listening to my banker as he pointed out historical landmarks like the UCLA campus, Rodeo Drive, and the Bel Air Country Club. He casually described his wealthy lifestyle as if it were normal for everyone. I thought why does wealth seem natural to some people and foreign to others?

The opulence of Beverly Hills was crazy to see. The streets were scattered with cars that cost more than the average American's annual salary. The shops were full of merchandise that only the ultra-rich could afford.

I wondered, how much money do you have to earn to be willing to buy a $300,000 car? Are these people just broke at a higher level, buying things to impress people they don't even care about? Are they living a fake lifestyle where the hood ornament on your car matters more than the character of the person driving it? Possibly, but maybe some of them know information about success that we do not know. Were these self-made people or were they living a lifestyle built by their parents?

I was willing to bet that not all these people inherited their wealth. According to Wikipedia in 2019 there were 18.6 million people with a net worth of more than $1,000,000.00. That is the highest rate the world.

There is opportunity everywhere if we can learn the secrets of the wealthy and be willing to do the work! Just two blocks away from Beverly Hills the streets are littered with tents and cardboard shanties. The sidewalks are full of garbage and waste.

Currently there are over 70,000 homeless people living on the streets of Los Angeles. Why did some end up living on the streets while others are living in Bel Air? What decisions did they make that led them in such different directions? What did they do, or not do that led them to where they are now? I have heard it said that we are all exactly where we deserve to be based on the sum-total of our decisions, can this be true?

Throughout my journey in life I have been blessed to learn valuable lessons that answer these questions. Some answers I learned from other people's experience and some I had to learn the hard way. I hope to share throughout these pages practical ideas and proven techniques on how you can master mediocrity.

That day in Beverly Hills my team was preparing to meet with two different billion-dollar companies to discuss business opportunities. I was there with my amazing daughter, the VP of Surveillance Systems Inc., our Northern California based, family owned, security company.

We had grown from an unknown start-up to one of the most well-known and largest gaming-centric security integration companies in North America.

Melissa is one of my closest confidants and I have the upmost love and respect for her. I am so blessed to have a daughter who has always inspired me to be a better man. We whispered to each other "Is this really happening, how the heck did we get here?" It was a surreal moment as the previous eighteen years in business flashed through my mind.

We had struggled and fought our way to gain visibility in a very narrow, extremely competitive space. SSI is a family and I had dreamt about all of us winning together for years. Thoughts of self-doubt slipped into my mind as I waited for the largest security company in the world to enter the room and take their seats on the opposite side of this massive conference table. I had butterflies in my stomach and sweat trickled down my body as I visualized how the meeting would flow. This was it, game time!

Many years ago, I learned that fear is good and if something scares you then it is probably the right thing to do. My senses were at a heightened state as I prepared to enter the arena. I reminded myself that even though tens of millions of dollars may be at stake, these are people just like everyone else.

They too, must go home at night and deal with their own personal issues. Behind closed doors we all have our own dark battles to fight. Nobody has greater value than you or me regardless of their title, hood ornament or address. We should never feel intimidated by anybody in business or in life.

As I sat waiting to present, I realized despite my life circumstances, I had done some things well enough to get me to this moment. The thought occurred to me that regardless of the outcome of this meeting, I wanted other people to know that they too can do anything I have done

The chapters to follow trace my life's journey as I learned to master mediocrity. As I talk about the highs, lows and all the craziness in between we are going to look at the ingredients that make a successful family, entrepreneur, and business.

CHAPTER 1

GROWING UP

GROWING UP IT DID NOT TAKE LONG FOR ME TO REALIZE that there were plenty of people that were more talented, better looking, and wealthier than me. I was an undersized kid growing up in a small town where everyone knew everyone else and there was a good chance you were somehow related.

Lincoln California was home to roughly 10,000 people, a high percentage of whom were multi-generational residents. Many of the kids I started kindergarten with would be a part of my graduating class 12 years later. My father was one of the small-town barbers. In those days the barber shops, beauty parlors, bars and churches were the social media of the community.

Business ownership was part of my family's DNA. In the 1950s my grandparents owned and operated a Flying A service station on Lincoln's main drag. My father and uncle worked there all through high school. The pictures looked like every movie I've seen that was set in the 50's, cool cars and good times. Later in his life my father would start his barber business on main street in the same small town.

After graduating from high school my dad followed my uncle Butch and enlisted in the Army. My uncle was stationed in beautiful Hawaii and my father was stationed in Germany on the freezing cold Czech border. My father still hates snow and often shares stories of his adventures in Europe, most of which include women, drinking and fighting.

After serving in the Army my father returned to Lincoln where he met and married my mother Iris Sharron Sims. My mother was a local beauty queen who came from humble beginnings, daughter of my Oklahoma, "Grapes of Wrath" grandparents, Riley and Floyce Sims.

Mom was Miss Placer County which qualified her to run for Miss California. I still tease my father to this day asking what he did to convince my mother to date him. My mother not only had the looks, but she was also a talented artist.

Bob and Iris Flowers would give birth to two boys, Robert and Todd. My parents would only remain married for a couple years and later I would discover that I was the result of rebound sex. That's good for self-image!

Today we live in a world of fake heroes and people who are famous for doing nothing. To me the real heroes are the moms and dads who do whatever it takes to take care of their children. My hero is my father who at the age of 29 took custody of his two boys and was determined to raise them to the best of his ability.

One day my mother showed up at his door with a frying pan and two little kids and said "good luck" she then turned and walked away leaving us behind. My dad was going to need to learn how to cook, but who needs a frying pan when you have Hungry Man frozen dinners? I always loved the hot molten lava apple pie desert that if eaten too quickly, would blister your mouth.

I was a true daddy's boy and would do anything for his approval. Our life as three bachelors was fairly decent but thank God for my grandma Hazel who would come stay with us often. She would make us special meals and treats allowing us a glimpse of what a normal life was like. I loved her with all my heart. She was my angel.

My brother Robert was always very athletic and consistently made the baseball all-star team. He was a natural artist and would paint Christmas murals from memory on the local store windows for extra money. He was also very smart and was named valedictorian for his eighth-grade graduation ceremony.

I remember listening to him practicing his speech on the topic of integrity. It was the first time I had ever heard the word which would later become a principle that guided me through very difficult times. I was literally the opposite of my brother in many ways.

I was born premature on November 13th, 1963, go Scorpios! In the 1960s Tetracycline was used to treat premature babies. One of the side effects of Tetracycline was that it darkened baby teeth and would occasionally stain permanent teeth.

So, there I was, an undersized boy with big ears and black teeth from a divorced family in a small town. I wasn't naturally gifted at anything and nothing would come easy for me. I was a "C" student and a mediocre athlete, destined to live a life of struggle.

I was teased daily, often from my own brother. It is interesting how the human mind works. I could have easily been crushed by my circumstances as many people are, but somehow my circumstances would become my fuel.

It is human nature to compare our weaknesses against other people's strengths resulting in negative feelings and depression. In today's world we are inundated by social media where people are posting snapshots of themselves living their best life while many are home feeling mediocre by comparison. The truth is most of what we see is false advertising.

People are attempting to create an illusion of who they are and the successes they have, perpetuating a false image of who they really are. They experience the endorphin rush of getting likes on their posts giving them a false sense of self-esteem. People are becoming increasingly desensitized to reality.

Many have become addicted to the opinions of people they do not even know. Social media has become the bathroom wall of society. Depression in the US is an epidemic and I believe it is the result of people who have lost sight of their self-worth through comparison.

There was no way I was going to allow myself to be a bullied bench warmer eating the scraps of society. I learned then a key principle that would change my life forever. What you lack in talent, you can make up for through sheer effort. I love a "hard tryer." This is a person who is willing to do whatever it takes, for as long as it takes, regardless of their circumstances.

As an eight-year-old this was not a cerebral epiphany, it was a necessity. It was a fire that started to burn in my soul. If I were picked on, I would fight back. Nobody wants to get punched in the face, not even a bully.

Now don't get me wrong, I wasn't a scrapper looking to get into fights, I just decided that the pain of a bloody lip was better than feeling like a loser. As a matter of fact, I quickly learned that skillfully used words could be as effective as a well-placed punch.

I started to develop my style of humor that combines some stinging truth with a funny punchline, which is still effective today. I'm not promoting sarcasm as a communication tool, but it seems to work for me.

CHAPTER 2

BUILDING MY BELIEF SYSTEM

"AS A **MAN THINKETH** IN HIS HEART, **SO IS HE**" PROVERBS 23:7 Whatever it is we spend all our time thinking about will manifest into our belief system.

One of my favorite mottos for living life is "time will either promote you or it will expose you" which holds true for everything we do including how we think.

Our thoughts create our belief system and our belief system determines our actions. Our actions compounded over time determine the kind of family life we have, the health of our relationships, our physical fitness, our relationship with God, our finances and lifestyle.

One of the most important, if not the most important, are the thoughts we have about ourselves and the impact they have on our self-esteem and self-worth.

How do we learn to think the way we think? There is no question in my mind that the way we are raised, and our environment helps mold who we are as adults.

I have seen within my own family that kids who have been raised in the same environment can be very different from each other. Why is it that siblings who are raised in the same environment are so unique from one another? Although these siblings may have had the same parents, grew up in the same house, and went to the same school, their personalities are dynamic and unique.

With the addition of each child, parents must adapt to parenting multiple children which alters the existing child-parent relationship. Now you add the age differences of the children and their unique personalities, the interpersonal relationship of each sibling will be different with each other and both parents.

Of course, these relationships have an impact on how these siblings think and how they process situations ultimately molding their self-esteem and behavior. I recognize that there are many different contributors that influence a child's self-esteem, but for my story I am focusing on the dysfunction that comes from broken homes, alcoholic parents, and abuse. These are all part of my childhood and were very important in developing how I think.

For some people, these dysfunctions drive them to succeed, while others hold on to their past and allow those same negatives to be their mantra for failure. Changing the mindset of a victim mentality person is extremely challenging if that person does not first decide to break free of the mental chains that are holding them down.

There are countless books and movies about people who have overcome tremendous odds to build incredibly successful lives despite their childhoods. Who doesn't love the story of the under-dog who finds a way to win in life?

We have also seen the tragic stories of people who overcome the odds to build what seems to be a happy, successful life, just to throw it all away with drugs, alcohol or even suicide. Have you ever wondered, what is going on inside these people's heads, why do they keep doing such stupid self-destructive things? How do you slip to such a dark place?

They can seem upbeat and happy when they are around, but when they are alone with their thoughts, they are miserable and depressed, suffering through each hour of every day looking for ways to numb the pain.

After my mother and father divorced, she married Frank Medrano and together they had four more children: Cindy, Tony, Peter, and Danny. They bounced around a little before settling in a small house in Grass Valley, CA.

Frank worked in the grocery business and mom worked in housekeeping at the local hospital. They seemed to work hard during the week, however when the weekends rolled around, they partied just as hard.

My parents shared custody and I would visit my "other" family every other weekend. I always looked forward to the time with my brothers and sister and we always had a great time being kids. I always felt loved, however at the same time I always felt like an outsider.

I felt guilty when I was with my father because I missed my mom and siblings, but when I was there with them, I felt guilty that I was not at home with my dad.

It was not uncommon for my mom and Frank to leave the kids with me while they went out to the bars. They frequented many of the same places, so I had a general idea where they were at any given time. I hated the fact that when I came to visit, they would leave.

I remember looking at the clock knowing the bars closed at 2:00 a.m. wondering when they would be home. Sometimes we would get scared being home alone and I would start calling the bars looking for my mother. Half the time I could not track her down. It made me feel terrible that she rarely saw me and when she did, she would prefer to go out rather than show me some semblance of a normal family life.

The challenge was once they returned, we knew we had better pretend to be asleep rather than feel the wrath of drunk Frank's violent nature

Although he never laid a hand on me, he would cut loose on my brothers with a belt. It was a horrifying sound to hear that big, leather belt as it struck them over and over. The sounds they made as they were beaten terrified me and kept the rest of us frozen as to not draw his attention. I hated it and could not wait to go home to my dad, yet I always felt tremendously guilty leaving the kids behind.

As I look back at my life, for as long as I can remember, all I wanted was a normal family, whatever that means. The lessons we can learn from our parent's mistakes or the mistakes of others can be incredibly influential on our dreams and goals in a very positive way, while for others it becomes a model to live by, that creates an unbroken chain of negativity.

I want to share several quick stories that had a tremendously positive impact on my life and that have helped fuel my desire to build my own family.

When my older brother Robert was eleven years old, I was eight, Cindy was five, Tony three and Pete two (Danny wasn't born yet) we were all together at a house my mom and Frank were renting in Marysville.

My mother and Frank told us that they had some errands to run and instructed me and Robert to keep an eye on the younger kids. A few hours passed and hunger set in. We scrounged through the empty cupboards and the refrigerator and found enough random food to shake the hunger pains. More hours passed and we began to worry. It was also dark, we were all getting hungry, cranky, and scared.

Since it was fairly normal for those two to hit a bar on their way home, I broke out the phone book and started canvassing their normal joints. Maybe that is where I learned to get over the fear of cold calling for business?

After calling every place and everyone we could think of, the littlest kids were falling asleep, so we made them comfortable and tried to make it fun. Robert and I stayed awake all night talking about what we should do. We knew the right thing to do was to call my father to come get us, however we were very worried what that would mean for the others. We could not abandon our sister and brothers.

I believe one of the best traits I have developed as a leader and entrepreneur is to keep emotions low and always look for a positive solution. I believe the birth of these skills came out of the purest of necessity, survival.

When we woke up the next day and our mother and father were nowhere to be found, Robert and I had to keep everyone at ease and make them feel safe. We turned on cartoons so they could be distracted while we hatched a plan to feed them.

A few blocks away there was a supermarket. Our strategic plan was to take all the little ones with us and have them run a distraction in the toy section while Robert and I shoplifted food. We understood that the store clerks would assume we were with our parents, since nobody sends five little kids to the store alone. My brother led us into action.

"Todd you hit the deli section, Cindy you take the littlest ones to the toys and act natural" which meant go raise cain while I go for milk and cereal. "Meet in the lobby in three minutes, go!"

We all went our separate directions and executed the plan with military precision. We circled back and met in the front lobby and exited through the doors used to bring in the shopping carts. We scurried back to the house with our little hearts beating out of our chests like we just pulled off the heist of the century.

Looking back, I know the Lord had to be helping us because how did nobody notice us leaving with our hands full of groceries? We had no way to conceal the merchandise. We were little kids with little kid's clothes.

Once back at the house Robert took inventory as we all huddled around our haul. We had milk, cereal, baloney, bread and of course cookies. We were kids, so of course we would get cookies instead of broccoli. With bellies full of breakfast, we were able to distract ourselves by watching TV and had no choice but to wait it out. By this time, we were incredibly worried, but we still had to keep our cool.

To this day I still get a pit in my stomach thinking about this. Morning turned into evening and we were all hungry again and stress levels were very high. I give Robert so much credit for doing whatever he could to make things seem normal. To have a nice warm dinner, he took the baloney from the package and began to fry it.

I had never seen this done before and I'm sure I complained that he was ruining our food. He used the fried baloney to make sandwiches and there was enough for seconds! I would have never dreamed that a fried baloney sandwich could taste so delicious.

Night came and went with still no word from our mother. It was time for desperate measures. Robert and I reluctantly called our father. Naturally, he lost his mind with anger and took immediate action. We told dad we were not going to leave these kids alone and for him to please help all of us. My dad rounded up my mom's sister, Aunt Hester, who lived nearby. A few hours later, our families showed up in force.

We all went our own way, me and Robert with my dad and the rest of the kids went with our Aunt Hester. My heart broke as I left my siblings behind, but I knew they would be safe, plus Aunt Hester made the best peach cobbler! Mom and Frank were tracked down later that day and had been on a three-day drunken bender.

Who in their right mind would abandon their kids like that? As an adult, that's a question I still ponder. Who in their right minds would do that? How can people have kids just to do terrible things to them? When I hear stories of child abuse or worse, it infuriates me to my core.

My one true prejudice in life is disdain towards people who choose to have kids and then do not care for them. I also recognize that I do not fully understand the human psyche and what has happened to these people to make them like they are. As such, I give my mother forgiveness and grace today because I have no idea what happened to her to make her the way she was.

My grandparents were wonderful people, but did my mother experience a traumatic event I don't know about or was it the compound effect of her negative thoughts that drove her to make such terrible mistakes?

At the same time, my mother could be very affectionate and loving. How would the craziness impact the development of her children as they mature into adults? We all had our own difficulties, but I consider myself the lucky one. I lived with my father, so I had an escape from the turmoil of two alcoholic parents.

Out of six kids, three have led normal, successful lives while three followed in her footsteps. Let me be very clear, the three of us who have lived normal lives had to deal with our own set of issues, but it's how we chose to handle those challenges that made the ultimate difference.

The other three chose to deal with their issues with drugs, alcohol, and crime, while blaming the world for their problems. The oldest had to join the Army and flee the country after stealing a suitcase of pills and powder from a neighborhood drug dealer who put out a contract on his life.

Another went to federal prison for statutory rape. The saddest story is that of our youngest brother who victimized himself by completely blaming my mother for every poor decision he's made while doing exactly what she had done.

Drugs and alcohol consumed his life and at one point he was living in the streets. He has struggled his entire life and has been in and out of jail promising sobriety. He had two children that he abandoned, making the circle complete.

My sister Cindy has done an amazing job raising herself while trying to help take care of her brothers. At age sixteen she had three jobs while cheerleading in high school.

I really do not feel that I have baggage from my childhood and my coping mechanisms have served me well as an adult. Now I'm sure that most people would say that the traumas of my childhood should be discussed with a professional who can help me navigate my thoughts, but at the same time these traumatic events have helped mold me into a father and husband who is tremendously passionate about his family. I have chosen to bury the negatives and never visit them unless I feel they can serve me in a positive way.

We all have enough to deal with in our daily lives and the last thing we need to do is saddle ourselves with the baggage of our own past failures or the mistakes of our parents.

It is obvious when you see people that succumb to the weight of their baggage. They are dragging the heavy luggage behind them full of the garbage of the past. Their shoulders are slumped, and their heads are down avoiding eye contact. They move slowly through life dragging the bags of garbage behind them leaving a wake of negativity. They blame the world for their problems and never hold themselves accountable. They contribute little to society, but feel the world owes them everything.

People that have a victim mentality develop a strong sense of entitlement. Rather than building a long-lasting career and being a contributor to society, they prefer to live off the government.

To them, the world owes them reparations for the struggles they had to endure growing up, and assume that everybody else has had it better. They say things like "those guys are so lucky" not realizing that luck had nothing to do with it.

I have chosen, right or wrong, to keep all my past garbage buried where it belongs. I refuse to be held hostage by my past mistakes or the mistakes of other people that I had no control over.

I also remember a certain Friday afternoon. I was super excited to see my mom and other family. I was six years old sitting in class, thinking about how much I missed my mom, brothers, and sister. When the school bell rang, I jumped up and ran all the way home to our yellow apartments just a few blocks away.

I jammed some clothes in a paper grocery bag and sprinted down the stairs down to the curb, and anxiously awaited my mother. It was two o'clock in the afternoon and I could feel the spring sun blazing down on me. I thought about running up to get a drink, but I didn't want to miss the look on my mother's face when she saw me. I just knew in my heart that she must be missing me the same way I was missing her. I could picture her crying at night wondering how and what I was doing.

I knew it must be brutal on her to miss out on all the memories I was making with my father. I just wished they were together.

Instead of leaving me for one or the other, we could have dinner at a dinner table and share stories together of what we did that day, just like I saw on TV.

My mind wandered as the minutes passed. Where was she? Did something happen to her? Was she in a car wreck? My day-dreaming of spending time with her turned to worry and fear. Hours passed.

The sun began to set, and the light dimmed around me. I sat there numbed with a sense that this day would turn out different than I had wanted. In the darkness I felt the gentle hand of my father on my shoulder. He led me back inside and assured me we would find out where she was.

As it turned out she made a pit stop at a local dive bar, the Weeping Willow. There was no way my dad was going to let me get in the car with a drunk. Even to this day I can still feel how deeply sad I was to know my mother would rather spend time with a bunch of losers instead of me. I swore at six years old that when I had kids, I would never do that to them.

I was always envious of my friends that had moms waiting at home for them. I often wondered what it would be like to have a full-time mom.

One afternoon, after school, I was playing with Kenny. He lived a few houses away from us across an open field behind my dad's house.

His mother called us in to have a snack. When I came through the back door into their kitchen, the house was filled with the smell of chocolate chip cookies baking in the oven. Sitting on the kitchen table were two plates of freshly baked, hot out of the oven, chocolate chip cookies, and two glasses of ice-cold milk.

As I sat with my friend, eating these amazing cookies, I thought to myself, "this is what it must be like to have a mother."

My kids will never have to wonder what it feels like to have a mother or a father. My kids will never have to wonder where I am or what I am doing. They will never feel lonely or abandoned. I will never make my kids feel like they are less important to me than anything else in my life.

I've only shared this story with a few people, and some of the people closest to me have never heard it before, but when I have, I've heard reactions like, "that's terrible" or "that's so sad." I'm sure at the time I felt lonely and sad, but this experience was molding my priorities. I thank God to this day that rather than dwelling on self-pity I made this my battle cry for parenting.

I will always be grateful to my mother for such strong life lessons, and I will always be thankful for my father who helped me understand those painful lessons. Those lessons became anchor moments in my life. They drove me to create the best possible life for my wife and kids. My prayer was for God to bless me with a strong wife and mother who is equally committed to our family and He did.

We all have stories of events that occurred in our childhoods that were traumatic. I bet you can remember some in vivid detail, like they happened yesterday. One of my mentors in life, Wade Simmons, taught me this valuable principle: it's not what happens to you in life, but it's how you choose to respond that really matters.

How we respond to life's challenges is based on our belief system, our programming and how we are wired. If this is true, and I know it is, that means we can alter how we think which will change our belief system and how we respond. We can literally rewire ourselves to live happy, successful lives!

We are in control, not the world. We get to determine our own outcomes. I was introduced to the power of positive thinking many years ago.

I learned that five years from now you will be like the people you associate with, the books you read and the recordings you listen to. I employed these success principles decades ago and I am living proof that you too can change.

Your belief system influences your actions, so how and what you think about will have a significant impact on your mental approach to getting the most out of life. Many of us were taught to get a good education, get a good job and work hard. Then, go buy a house, get married, and live happily ever after.

But what I witnessed was that a lot of people were living mediocre lives, struggling from paycheck to paycheck. I realized that there are those who have it, and those who don't.

What you lack in talent you can make up for with hard work, but the world is filled with miserable hard-working people. Sometimes in life ignorance is not bliss. Knowledge is power and once I was exposed to new information, I was shocked to find that there was a plethora of books, recordings, and information from authors and speakers who teach how to think differently.

Some of my favorite books and authors on positive thinking are *Think and Grow Rich* by Napoleon Hill, *The Magic of Thinking Big* by David Schwartz and *What to Say When You Talk to Yourself* by Shad Helmstetter.

In fact, there is an entire multi-billion-dollar industry built on teaching and sharing this information. How is it that I grew up and never heard anything about this? The power of positive thinking was never taught in school. I never heard it from my parents, coaches, or anyone else.

The way you think and what you confess can help you live a life full of joy and happiness but can also have a devastating impact on your life. As I sit here writing this chapter my family is planning the funeral and mourning the loss of my younger sister-in-law Julie who recently died a tragic death. She physically died last week but mentally she died ten years ago.

To be clear, the content of this book is based only on my personal life experiences and I make no claims to be an expert on the human psyche. With that said I can also say that it does not take a genius to recognize somebody who displays self-destructive behavior.

It does not take a PhD to recognize somebody who is so deeply depressed that they are only a shell of who they once were. It truly breaks my heart to think that there are people who feel they have no self-worth, no value to the world, and that are just willing to fade away.

Despite many struggles during my childhood, I still learned many vital lessons. Another arena of my childhood that served as a backdrop for learning life lessons came in form of sports.

CHAPTER 3

HEART OVER TALENT

IF I WANTED A STARTING POSITION ON THE BASEBALL team I would have to practice longer and harder than the rest of the team. When I started playing Little League, we lived in a second story two-bedroom apartment. My father would take me downstairs every night, position me right in front of a wooden picket fence, and fire rockets at me until I conquered my fear of the ball.

The pain of getting hit with the ball was far better than the embarrassment of striking out in front of a crowd. Often, when I missed the ball, it would knock the pickets off the fence. As time went on, I became a fairly decent baseball player with a consistent bat and a few times I found my way to the all-star team.

I am sure my father did not realize at the time that his lessons on overcoming fear would help me as a salesperson and later as a business owner. Years later, when I was twelve years old, I was playing baseball for a great little league team, the Braves. I was in majors for three years, and all three years we won the championship.

Our team was invited to play in a regional tournament of champions in a town about an hour away in Nevada City, an old historical gold rush town. Our first opponents would be the Nevada City hometown champions.

When we arrived at the ball field my heart was racing with excitement. We were proudly wearing our new TOC jerseys and hats, it felt really good to be a part of something special. Both teams gathered in our dugouts looking across the field to measure up the competition.

There was a kid in their dugout that was two feet taller than the rest, and from across the field we could even see his facial hair. We just figured he was a young assistant coach. The umpire called our team to the field to warm-up.

The visiting team always took the field first. We went through our normal warm-up fielding some grounders while allowing our pitcher to get some throws in, all part of our normal routine.

After about ten minutes the umpire called us off so the home team could warm-up. Once the home team warmed-up they would remain on the field and we would start the game. I went to the dugout and grabbed a helmet and carefully chose my bat. Like every hitter, I had my go-to favorite. I was the number two batter in the line-up. I had developed into a very solid hitter and always seemed to find a way to first base.

I stood near our dugout taking some warm-up cuts with the bat as their pitcher took the mound to get his throws in. I could not believe my eyes. It was the giant man-child we had seen in the dugout! Our team fell silent as we watched him prepare to throw the ball.

The beast went through a slow, casual wind up and released the ball. It looked like a white beam of light permeating from his hands leaving a trail like a meteorite. Then like a crack of light-ening, it hit the catcher's mitt with a blistering pop. Our coach could see the looks of concern clearly visible all over our faces, so he did what any good coach would do, he tried to inspire us with false hope.

"The harder they throw, the further you hit it" barked our old scruffy coach. He looked like a miniature version of Abraham

Lincoln as he delivered his pregame speech, knowing he was sending us to the trenches to die. I refused to die, but I was definitely feeling the fear.

The umpire called out our first batter, Dean Cooper. He was a tall, lanky country boy that I shared the catcher's position with. Dean took his place in the batter's box. Our team cheered as the pitcher went into his wind-up. He released his pitch with fury. In a split-second the pitch hit Dean in the head sending him crashing down.

Dean was not moving as our coach rushed to his aid. Dean continued to lay there not moving. The pitch had knocked Dean unconscious, a one punch knockout! I could hear our crowd yelling at the umpire to check the pitcher's birth certificate.

The onsite paramedics came to deliver first-aid to Dean. They loaded him on a stretcher and hauled him off to the hospital. The good news was Dean only had a concussion and was soon released.

Our coach retuned to the dugout. I was standing in the on-deck circle like a statue, as white as a ghost. Our coach threw Dean's helmet in the garbage, the projectile had split it in half.

"Batter up" the umpire yelled. I looked up into the stands for some reassurance from my father. He looked back and gave me the ol' reaffirming nod. I set my jaw, clinching my teeth together.

As I approached the batter's box, I stared down the pitcher every step of the way, sending him a clear message that I was not to be intimidated. I looked confident on the outside, but I was dying on the inside. I raised my hand up to the umpire to call time while I dug my back foot into the soil, reassuring I could drive the ball with power. The man-child looked at me and grinned. My heart sank, but there was no way I was going to give him the glory. I was afraid I was going to pee my white pants. There was nowhere to hide.

He went into his slow wind up and I responded by slowly leaning backwards. I had to time my moves perfectly, so I didn't give away my plan of retreat. Just at the moment he released the pitch, I threw myself out of the box in search of safe ground.

"Strike one!" the umpire yelled. Once again, I looked at my father for advice. "Don't bail out of the box. You got this Ty, you got this." My father had nick named me Tyrone, different story, different time.

I reentered the box, once again digging it. This would prove to be an anchor moment in my life. There will be many times in life when we will all be forced to face our fears. Would I learn to accept that it's OK to bail out of the box when times get tough, or would I learn to face my fears and take action? I decided at that moment that I would rather feel the pain of getting beaned than live with the humiliation of giving up.

He went into his wind-up. It was like watching a slow-motion replay until he released the pitch. In a millisecond it looked like it would be a strike, so I turned the bat as fast as I could, making solid contact with the ball sending it over the fence. No, it wasn't a home run, it was a foul tip that banged off the metal roof of the snack bar.

The crowd cheered as I re-approached the box, repeating the same routine as always. Tap the bottom of my bat against my cleats, step in the box digging in my rear foot, and take my stance ready to conquer the pitch.

He wound up and delivered another rocket. It wildly soared near my head hitting the wooden back stop with such force, everyone in the park could hear the sonic boom. I scowled at the pitcher shaking my head in disgust, thinking to myself "If that thing hits me in the face, I'll be disfigured for life."

One ball, two strikes. My father had taught me another valuable life lesson, always go down swinging. I was not going to just stand there and take the third strike, and then be forced to take the walk off shame back to the dugout.

He released the pitch and it looked like another strike. Once again, I gave it all I had. I felt my bat make contact with the ball, but the pitch happened so fast I could not see it. I dropped my bat and started to sprint towards first base when I heard the umpire yell "batter out!"

I had foul tipped the ball right into the catcher's glove. For some reason, striking out did not feel like losing. I had not achieved my goal of getting a base hit, yet I did not feel like a failure. I faced my fears like a man, and in my heart, I knew I had given it my best shot.

We lost the game; however, I won an important life lesson. I would rather try and fail, than never try at all. People who know me well have heard me say "I love a hard trier." I will always back someone who is willing to do their best to succeed. I will take heart over talent any time.

CHAPTER 4
WHATEVER IT TAKES

NECESSITY IS THE MOTHER OF ALL INVENTION. MY DAD taught me one of my life's most valuable lessons. If you want money go find a way to earn it. At the time I just thought he was a cheapskate.

My friend's parents would just give them money when they wanted it so why did I have to go earn it? Because I was just a kid, I was oblivious that we were living off his receipts of the day, as he struggled to make it as a new business owner.

As an adult I understand the tremendous pressure he was under every single day of trying to pay a mortgage and put food on the table while trying to build his customer base.

If I wanted spending money, I would have to get creative. I looked around the house at the tools I had at my disposal, there wasn't much to choose from. One item jumped out at me though. Our old, beat up, Snapper lawn mower. I decided to push the mower around the block searching for lawns with tall grass.

I would muster up the courage, practice my sales pitch, and knock on the front door of houses whose lawns needed a trim. I'm sure some of the neighbors just felt sorry for me, but most praised my ambition even if their answer was "no." It was encouraging and I realized it was a only numbers game and I only need one "yes" to change my day! The single yes far outweighed the many rejections.

Over the years I knocked on their doors many times selling things like garden seeds, magazines, fundraisers, contests, or anything else that I could make a buck on.

Nothing wrong with a pity sale, or even dealing with the occasional grumpy old man, I was learning how to win in sales. I experienced a very powerful lesson. When we are willing to do the things in life others are not willing to do, we can live a life they will never have. This helps us master mediocrity. I was willing to do whatever it would take to succeed. I am eternally grateful for the best teacher in my life, my father. He always supported me. As time went on, I figured out new ways to make money. I worked on a local farm building fences like a junior ranch hand. I had a part-time job working for my dad's best buddy at his lawn mower sales and repair shop. It was a filthy job, but I loved being around my dad's crew.

When I was a sophomore in high school, a couple friends and I were offered temporary jobs in a grocery store. The local grocery union had gone on strike and we were offered the opportunity to make some extra money.

We naively accepted not fully understanding what it meant crossing the picket line during a strike. That was a crazy and unique experience. We made fantastic money and I loved the experience. The man who offered us the job was a neighbor to my best friend Mike, his name is Don Baxter, and he is still my life-long friend.

What Don did not know is that I had a crush on his daughter Marcy. I wanted to spend every moment I could with her and soon found myself hanging around their house every day.

In the beginning Don put up with me hanging around and Marcy's mother Rosalyn made me feel welcome. Don delivered a clear message to me very early in our relationship. "Marcy is my baby girl, so if you do anything to hurt her, I will have to blow your head off." What I did not know was an hour earlier he had spotted me driving like a mad man with her in my dad's gigantic Pontiac Bonneville!

I worked very hard to gain Don's approval and I figured out his likes and dislikes. Although he never said it, I believe we were kindred spirits because we both shared similar childhoods. I knew how to cook and clean and was not afraid of hard work, he respected that about me.

Don did not accept excuses only results. Do what you say you're going to do and do it to the best of your ability. Their family became like the family I never had. For the first time in my life I was experiencing the daily life of a complete family.

Looking back as an adult, I realize I was young and needy and had to be a real pain since I was at their house seven days a week, but Don had a solution in the form of opportunity.

My junior year in high school Don got me a job with at an old school, Italian owned, grocery chain named Corti Brothers. It was a high-end store with a full-service deli and meat department complete with imported food and wine.

My job was to work weekend evenings cleaning the deli after the store closed. It was a dirty job, but it felt amazing to receive a check with my name on it. I would drive home late at night smelling of deli meat and sweat but I loved every minute of it.

I worked hard for the money, but I also wanted the approval of Don, my father, and anyone else who was looking. With Don's coaching and unconditional accountability, I quickly advanced and was promoted to the grocery department.

After football season I worked 20 hours a week and full time in the summer. After graduating in 1981, I can recall experiencing my first forty-hour work week and how long the days seemed. Two, ten-minute breaks and a lunch hour was not enough time to make up for having the entire summer off to do whatever I wanted.

I hated the feelings of confinement. It was like serving a prison sentence, but I was making great money for a kid. More importantly I was learning to become a man. Don was very happy with my performance and continued to fast-track me to management, and why not, I was going to be his future son-in-law.

I was getting a great start in life, however I was unsatisfied and wanted more. Little did I know that my ignorance of delayed gratification would cause me some real heartache. I had no idea how to reach my dreams and goals, but I did understand the value of a strong work ethic.

Chapter 5

CHAMPAGNE TASTE ON A BEER BUDGET.

Growing up in a small town like Lincoln I started to realize that the standard expectation was to get married young, buy a small house, get a good job and work forever just to pay bills. I did not want a life of working to just get by. There had to be something better. The people I knew who were living mediocre lives always came across as bitter and unhappy, they lived for Friday.

I love the outdoors and have always enjoyed camping, but I had dreams of traveling the world not spending one week a year in a campground. Let me be clear, in no way am I judging people who camp often, I still do. I just did not want sleeping on the hard ground in a tent to be my only form of vacation. I have many family members and friends who are living happy lives like this, but at that time in my life I was very uneasy with the status quo and I wanted more than a normal lifestyle.

I had dreams of a big house in the country with a loving wife and six kids. I wanted to drive exotic cars and travel the world. I wanted to eat in expensive restaurants and enjoy an uncommon lifestyle.

In reality, I had no idea how to get there or what it would take. I just figured if I would just work hard enough and long enough,

I would find a way. It is so funny, when my father would hear me talking about those things, he would always tell me that I had champagne taste on a beer budget. It came from a good place. He did not want to see me disappointed.

All my friends were headed off to college. Maybe getting a good education and a college degree would be the key to my future success, so I enrolled at the local Junior College. I had no clue what kind of career I wanted, but I was creative and a decent artist, so I decided I was going to major in marketing and advertising.

I enrolled in night classes so I could continue to work full-time during the day. I was prepared to take things seriously, since I was responsible for paying for my own education. When I walked onto the campus my heart was beating with anticipation of my new future! I sat in class listening to the instructor describing the curriculum and the calendar of the upcoming semester. She seemed a little bitter and her talk was uninspiring.

I sat there and thought "I already make more money than you." What was it she could possibly teach me that would take me closer to my dreams? At our first break, I ignorantly walked out of the class and left the campus, never to return. I regret not obtaining a degree. I was going to get my education the hard way, through real life experience.

Six years later I was the youngest assistant store manager in Corti Brothers history. Don had become a mentor and close friend. Most of the old cronies who were lifetime grocery clerks did not like me and called me a brown-noser.

They were happy doing mediocre work and any time there was a challenge, they were the first people to call on their union rep to protect them. They were just buying their time to retirement. However, I was super motivated working nights, weekends, and holidays, whatever paid the most. I was driving a brand-new Ford GT Mustang 5.0 and feeling proud.

My father had always preached to me to only buy cars I could pay cash for, and to do whatever it would take to remain debt free, but what did he know? It was common for me to have multiple uncashed payroll checks laying around my bedroom.

I still lived at home rent free with no other bills other than a car payment. I was rich. Every year I would take the money I had saved and against my father's coaching, I would run out and buy another new car. This was a bad habit that would have very negative ramifications in my near future.

I grew uneasy in my relationship with Marcy and decided to make a move. I found an apartment forty-five minutes away in Sacramento, closer to work. I wanted to get out of that small town and experience some new things closer to the clubs and action.

I handled the break-up like an immature, selfish kid. I felt like I had let her, and her entire family down. In retrospect I would have handled the situation much better than I did, but isn't that the case with many things?

My roommate had also been in a long-term relationship and he was also looking for a change. We were at a different happy hour every night and would close down the bars every Saturday night. I was probably going a little crazy with all this new freedom and was spending all my money on having fun.

It felt amazing to have my own place, but after taxes, rent, a car payment and partying I found myself living from paycheck to paycheck. The realities of adulthood were settling in quickly, but I was determined to party on. The attention I was getting from all those women was feeding all my mommy abandonment issues, but there was still something missing.

Parties and girls were not filling the hole in my heart and I was getting disenchanted with the whole scene. That would all change one Saturday night, April 1985 at a club called Confetti's. I strolled in like I had many times before like a lion looking for a helpless gazelle. The more drinks I had the more confident (stupid) I became. I had a simple, yet deadly strategy.

I would look around the bar and dance floor throughout the night. If a cute girl made eye contact and smiled. I would lock eyes and move slowly in her direction allowing her time to drink me in, one sip at a time.

"Would you like to dance?" If I got a yes, I would hold her hand to the dance floor where we allowed the music to move our souls, I would match her movements and be spiritually seductive. I would smile and stare into her eyes, dancing closer and closer, never breaking eye contact. These lucky girls never had a chance, or at least that is how I like to tell the story.

Here is the reality, I was there with my goofy friends drinking, dancing, and having a good time, just like we had many times before. I did meet a lot of girls and had a lot of fun. But it was getting old fast. I was a 21-year-old grocery clerk wearing white Levi's and cowboy boots. I had on my favorite, peach colored Le Tigre shirt, tucked in, of course. My hair was parted down the middle and feathered back to perfection. When I smiled the lights from the dance floor bounced off my mouthful of metal braces.

CHAPTER 6

WOMAN OF MY DREAMS

I HAD JUST LEFT THE DANCE FLOOR THIRSTY. I WAS standing at the bar enjoying a refreshing Long Island Iced Tea when my buddy Mike came up and told me he had just danced with the prettiest girl in the club and I asked him who it was.

We walked over and there she was, on the dance floor, dancing with another guy. This was unacceptable. That guy was dancing with the woman I would spend the rest of the night, I mean the rest of my life with. It was love, or something like love, at first sight. I had to meet this beautiful vixen right away.

The song ended so I had to move quickly. I had to serpentine towards her, dodging bodies like a hall of fame running back looking to score.

"Excuse me," I began.

"My friend just told me he had just danced with the most beautiful girl in here and he was right."

I set the hook and began to reel her in. I'm Todd, what is your name? "Lisa," she replied. I asked if she would please dance with me and thankfully, she said "yes."

I brought her to the dance floor and executed my strategy with precision, the smiling, the staring, while showing her all my sweet moves.

We danced for hours. I held her hand at the end of each song, warding off any potential predators. Over the course of the evening I was able to squeeze in a few key questions. At some point in my life I had heard that it is good to ask females questions and try to show genuine interest in their answers. This was not a skill that I would have learned from my father.

During the interrogation, Lisa said she was enrolled in college and was learning to be a legal secretary and that she had graduated from a high school near my hometown. She was a Del Oro Eagle.

Even though she had graduated from a school I despised because of the severe beatings I endured from their football program year after year, I couldn't take my eyes off her. Lisa was at the club with a girlfriend from school. She had just turned 21 and had never been to this club before. But here is where she made the big mistake, she told me she lived in Newcastle with her parents, an important detail I would not forget.

I knew I had to be with this amazing girl, so I strategically gave my car keys to my friend and told him I would ask her to give me a ride. It was getting late, so it was time to call it a night. I walked Lisa outside and asked her if she would like to see my new car.

She did not seem that impressed with my new Mustang since she had an original 1967 Z28 Camaro sitting at home. I told her my friends had taken off with my keys and asked if she would mind giving me a ride to my friend's house since it was on her way home.

She agreed, so we hopped in her car for the short ten-minute drive. I didn't have much time. I had to really lay on the charm if I had any chance of convincing her to stay the night with me.

We pulled up in front of his house and she left the car running. I pleaded with her to come in and hang out for a while, but she did not fall for my nice guy routine. Lisa explained why she didn't feel comfortable since we had just met, and she told me of her other priorities.

This made me respect her and now I wanted her even more. I asked if I could see her again and she said "yes." We would likely see each other at the club again. I kissed her cheek and we parted ways.

I could not stop thinking about her all weekend. What, not even a phone number? How was I going to track this girl down? I turned to the only internet we had at the time, the Placer County phone book.

How many people with the last name of Clark could possibly live in the town of Newcastle? There were a few so I decided I would implement the process of elimination. I started with Mr. Irwin D. Clark. I broke out my Thomas Bros. map guide and started my journey. I found my way to a country house nestled on four acres. I drove down the long drive and turned in to park.

I was met out front by a tall, slender man who was working in his garden. I asked him if he was Mr. Clark. He responded in the affirmative but said nothing more.

I'm sure he was wondering who I was. I asked him if he had a daughter named Lisa and again, he said yes but nothing further.

The silence was killing me, so I nervously told him that I was a friend of Lisa's and I was just stopping by for a quick visit. I was praying it would work out and I would not leave humiliated. No risk, no reward.

He told me the that he had just got home from work and the family was off at his other daughter's softball game, but I was more than welcome to wait. He pulled up a couple lawn chairs and offered me a cold beer. I made polite small talk with Irv while waiting for Lisa and her family to return.

Soon after, they rolled down the driveway. As the car came closer and their faces came into focus, I spotted Lisa behind the wheel. I could see the look of surprise on her face when she realized that this potential stalker from the bar was waiting at her home.

She and her family piled out of the car and instantly the decibel level went to a hundred. Apparently, Lisa's sister Julie was an assassin on the pitching mound, but a rival team had handed them a rare loss. I quickly introduced myself to her family knowing that if her father and her mother both liked me that I stood a much better chance with this girl.

Lisa was very surprised that I figured out where she lived and even more surprised that I was sitting talking with her father. Apparently, he did not like too many people, but he liked me. I told her that I could not stopped thinking about her and enthusiastically expressed my desire to see her again. We were embarking on a crazy journey together.

Lisa and I spent the next few months dating. We were both unsure of this new commitment which caused some relationship issues that we had to work through. Most of mine came from childhood insecurities. I had developed a distrust of most women that manifested in disrespect.

Lisa would be the woman who healed that hole in my heart. Lisa was and still is a beautiful woman, but most of all I was attracted to her strong family values. I wanted my children to experience life with a full time, loving mother. I was confident that together, we would be an unstoppable team. After just a few months of dating, I asked Lisa to marry me. Together we would build the family of our dreams. We were married on June 7th, 1986. And so, it began.

CHAPTER 7

BUILDING OUR DREAM

LISA AND I BOUGHT A NEW HOUSE THREE DOORS DOWN from my best friend and his wife, Mike and Dana Schwartz. It was an interesting friendship. Mike and I were inseparable.

We were friends all through high school. In fact, Mike introduced me to Marcy and the Baxter family in the first place. We had worked together in the grocery business for years, and later we worked together in the insurance business. Mike was also the guy who had danced with Lisa and pointed her out to me at the club. He was the best man in my wedding and now we were neighbors.

I was still working at Corti's while Lisa was hired as a legal secretary in the foster care department for the State of California. We both made decent money and had fantastic benefits. We lived in a new house and were driving new cars. I was proud of my new Snapper lawnmower that I would push around the yard once a week. It felt amazing.

We personified the young successful couple. We looked really good on the outside. The reality was, we were living from paycheck to paycheck, up to our ears in debt, and completely leveraged. We looked good and smelled good, but I was leading us right off a financial cliff.

I did not know how we were going to make ends meet. While it seemed like a logical idea at the time, we started using credit since cash was nonexistent. Soon, out of desperation, it got out of control.

We were piling on the debt using multiple credit cards at once. I knew I was violating every financial principle I had ever learned, but we were out of options. Delayed gratification made no sense to me when I could buy things today and pay for them tomorrow. I did not realize that the borrower is enslaved to the lender. I thought as long as we were making the monthly minimal payments that we were doing alright.

At the same time we were piling on the debt, we started having children. The timing was less than perfect but we really wanted to grow our family. I had no idea the expenses related to having babies. I figured that all they did in the beginning was eat, sleep, and go to the bathroom. Who knew that disposable diapers were made out of gold, so I suggested we use cloth diapers instead. Bad choice!

I told Lisa I was willing to do whatever it takes financially if she would agree. I dreamed of big family dinners, crazy holidays, and birthday parties. We would build the perfect family and all live happily ever after.

Lisa had only one requirement. She wasn't willing to allow someone else to raise our kids. She was either going to be a stay at home mom, or we were going to delay having children. Being the problem solver I am, I decided to resurrect my window cleaning business Don had encouraged me start many years earlier.

I was confident I could make enough money to replace Lisa's income. After taxes, gas, parking, new work clothes and lunches, her net income was only around $800 per month. We would just cut back on all entertainment and fun and I would spend all my off-time cleaning windows. Now that's a winning plan!

Lisa believed in me, so in the blink of an eye, she was somehow pregnant. It had to be immaculate conception because I don't even remember engaging in that type of activity.

If you have one baby, you might as well have three or four. Just a few short years later we achieved our well thought out plan. Our beautiful daughter Melissa is the oldest followed by two boys Michael and Austin. Masen would join the team six years later. He had to wait, Lisa was a little tired.

It was a sunny Friday afternoon when I arrived home from work. I pulled in the driveway and hopped out of my car to find my friend and neighbor Mike standing there waiting for me. What made that situation odd was we just worked the same shift and literally arrived home at the same time.

I said, "hey Mike what's up?" Normal conversation, right? What made it weird was his body language and his nervous response. He replied in a shaken voice, "Are you open to other ways of making money?" Not waiting for my response, he tossed a cassette tape at me, turned, and briskly started to walk away.

"Wait, what is this, what are you talking about? We were just at work together and you didn't say anything." He had moved even further away, so I had to yell "Hold on a minute, if this is Amway or something like that, don't waste my time."

I had no history with Amway or any other multi-level-marketing business. It was just a knee-jerk response to his ninja style approach. He was my best friend, so he felt comfortable responding with a, "just shut up and listen to this tape." He yelled back over his shoulder, "I'll need that back tomorrow so get on it."

I looked down. It was titled *Throw Away the Crutches* by Jim Floor. I had never heard of this guy, but Mike's approach intrigued me. He knew I was open to making more money. I was working full time. I had a window cleaning business and a wife who wanted to be a stay at home mom. I would go back to mowing lawns for my neighbors if it meant keeping her home with our kids.

I went straight in the house and listened to the thirty-minute recording. Jim Floor was a very enthusiastic speaker and I could tell that his talk had been recorded in front of a very excited, live audience. He described a lifestyle that I had always dreamed of.

He talked about the beautiful car, the big house in a gated community, fun vacations, and extra cash. What really caught my attention was when he talked about freedom. The freedom to do what you want, when you want, with who you want, without the constraints of time or money.

I wanted freedom! The only challenge was I missed the part where he told me how to achieve it, so I listened to the tape over and over and over, all night long. Then, I had Lisa listen to it with me so she could get excited about it too.

Although I was very skeptical, I was equally interested in learning more about this new opportunity. I had a tremendous amount of trust in Mike. If he was interested there must be something good there. Mike told me that he was in the same boat as me and really has no more information about this than me.

He had received the tape a few days earlier from our neighbor Ernesto and wanted to include me. Mike called Ernesto and informed him of our interest. Ernesto explained that he was working with Wade Simmons who would be more than happy to come to my house and explain the details of this mysterious business.

I didn't know much about Wade other than he had graduated from the same high school I went to. Wade had led the Lincoln varsity football team through an undefeated season and brought home the championship. He was also dating a beautiful cheerleader, Teri.

That was years prior and I had no idea what he had been up to since then. I told my father who was coming over to my house. He warned me to keep my guard up. He told me that Wade Simmons was a hustler and fairly egotistical. In retrospect, my dad was just doing his best to protect me from making a mistake.

Mike booked the appointment for Tuesday night at 8:00 pm. My suspicions were maxed out. Anyone I mentioned the tape and meeting to warned me against going and getting hooked into some pyramid scheme. I knew I was safe though since I had absolutely no money.

It is easy to listen to skeptics, but I had developed the mindset that unless you're paying my bills, I'm not going to listen to your negative opinion. There is always someone offering up their glass-half-empty outlook. Holy cow, why did the resounding messaging make me feel like people think I was an idiot? I started to get a little mad about all the unsolicited doubt and negativity.

Tuesday rolled around. Mike and I were both scheduled to work until 7:00 PM all the way in South Sacramento so I had to hurry to get home in time to scarf down some food before Wade arrived.

I broke a few speeding laws and arrived home at 7:45. I ran in the house and ate as fast as I could. There was a knock at the door. It was Mike, not Wade Simmons. Mike informed me that Wade was running late. I was furious

At 8:15 p.m. there was another knock on the door. In came Wade who immediately took charge of my house. Wade was dressed in a suit and tie, looking like a real businessman. He told us that it would be best if we could sit at the kitchen table. He told me to sit to his right and asked if Lisa could sit right across from him. At the time, I did not understand his strategy. Wade had a plan.

After a bit of small talk, Wade started asking us about our dreams and goals. He took us on a journey of possibilities. We talked about the kind of lifestyle we had always dreamed of. Lisa and I wanted a big house in the country on a beautiful piece of property. We expressed our strong desire to make enough money that Lisa would not have to work outside the home. We dreamed of beautiful vacations and time with our family. I soon realized what this guy was up to. He was getting us all juiced up so he could sucker us into his business.

Wade explained to us that there were only a few different ways people make money. Most people trade their time for money in a job or a small business. Since there are only so many hours you can work in a day, your income will always peak out.

You will either have a lot of time or you will have a lot of money, you will never have both. That is exactly where we were at the time. We were working hard, but our incomes were maxed out.

He told us we had to make a choice. We could either shrink down our dreams to match our incomes or we could find a way to increase our incomes to match our dreams.

I had seen what it looks like when people shrink their dreams and I did not want to live that way. He was setting his hook and slowly reeling us in. I was fully aware of what he was doing, but I was getting really excited.

Wade had the answer to how we could increase our incomes. He started talking about a business model that only required us to purchase products we had already been using and find a few customers to do the same. Everybody uses soap and toothpaste. How hard could this be?

He went on to explain the beauty of a business that is built on consumable products. When consumers run out of products they use every day, regardless of the economy, they buy them again. My mind was spinning out of control thinking about all the amazing things Lisa and I could do together. This was a husband and wife, home based business, something we could build together.

The business had a low start-up cost and offered a high return. The kicker was there were experienced people who were motivated to help us! Wade started drawing all these crazy circles. He said if you could find six motivated people, who find four, and those four find two that we could make $2000.00 every month!

Wade asked a key question. He asked, "Let's say that along the way you're only making $800 per month, what would you do with it?" I quickly responded with "I would buy a new ski boat!"

Under the table, Lisa swiftly kicked my shin causing me to react by crashing my knee into the table. I yelled "Hey, why did you kick me?" Wade looked startled. I'm sure he must have been thinking that he really had his hands on some winners here.

Wade turned from me and looked straight ahead and asked Lisa what she would do with the money. Lisa reasonably stated that she would use the money to pay our bills. I felt as though I was getting backed into a corner. I guessed that was what personal responsibility felt like.

Wade went on with the plan keeping his focus on Lisa. He understood that if the husband says yes to the business, but the wife is negative, it is a no go. But if the wife gets excited and says "yes," it is more likely they will join.

Help six people do what you did with the 6-4-2 and you could make $100K per year which blew my mind. I didn't know anybody who made $100K. It seemed so unreal. Build a network of people who use and sell products and we could get out of debt. All of this sounded incredibly easy and Wade promised to help us.

Wade wrapped up the plan by explaining that he belonged to two different organizations. One was a support team that would supply books, tapes, seminars and major events for teaching, training and motivation. This organization was named INA which stood for "International Networking Association." He wrote INA on pad of paper. I was incredibly pumped up.

Then he dropped the bomb! The second organization was our supplier who handled all the manufacturing of the product. The name of the company was, of course, Amway. I knew it. This all sounded too good to be true.

He went on to explain all the misconceptions about Amway and why some people had a negative impression of the company. I exhaled in disappointment with my head full of questions. My excitement was dwindling fast.

Wade went out to the car to retrieve some information. I turned to Mike who had sat silent during the entire meeting and asked him if he was going to do this thing. Mike said he was.

Wade came back through the door carrying a white cardboard box with handles. He explained that the box had some products to sample, some follow up tapes, and a couple of books. He took out a book titled *The Magic of Thinking Big* by David J. Schwartz.

He pointed out a few specific chapters to read like *Cure Yourself of Excusitis, the Failure Disease*. Do you have excuses to fail or reasons to succeed? Little did I know that this introduction to books would change the course of my life. He said he would pick up the box in a few days.

Wade was getting ready to leave but like any good salesperson he booked a follow up meeting. He and Mike left the house. Lisa and I looked at each other and smiled in disbelief. I told her that I had no intention of building a business like this, but I thought she would be good at it since she was so outgoing.

I had a thought that I could not get out of my mind. "What if Mike and Dana decided to build this business and we didn't?" If they were to become successful and we did not even try, I might have to kill my best friend. I could not allow them to leave us behind!

I placed the box of follow up material next to the couch where it would sit unopened until Wade came to pick it up. Why does it have to be called Amway? Why can't they call it something else? Our excitement was gone, replaced by doubt and fear.

Giving in to fear has never felt like winning to me. We had to remain open minded to new opportunities so we could get our debt under control. The money was enticing, but what the money could do for our family was more enticing. If we could replace Lisa's income, she could be a full-time, stay at home mom. This may be the chance we desperately needed to play financial offense for a change.

When Wade came back over, we let him know that I borrowed the $100 to sign up and get started from my Dad and we were ready to go. Lisa's only condition was that we were going to call it Yawma which is Amway spelled backwards, that way if the kids repeat it, nobody would know what we were doing.

We were completely broke, yet we were still worried what people might think. How many people hold themselves back from pursuing something new because they are worried about what people might think?

The reality is people don't think that much about you or me, they are spending all their time thinking about themselves. It's a funny thing when you try to step away from the herd, there's always someone there to pull you back in line.

Most people have an innate fear of change, so any time you choose to step out and do something to improve your life that makes them feel uncomfortable, you can expect negativity. It's a natural knee-jerk reaction.

Sometimes the negativity comes from the people who love you most and is disguised with well-meaning statements like "I just don't want to see you get hurt." There is no need for you to get defensive, just use it as motivation for you to succeed. Later, when they see that you didn't give up, they will be your biggest cheerleaders and tell you "I always knew you could do it."

Let me be clear, I am not suggesting that you join Amway or any other multi-level marketing business. However, it is a very important part of my story and has had a significant impact on who I am today.

It was the first time in my life that I was introduced to information promoting a different way of thinking, and promoting a positive mental attitude through books, audios, seminars, and association.

This was an opportunity for me to get an education while improving who I was as a human. You just don't know, what you don't know, until someone shines a light on you.

I continue to invest into personal growth and plan to do so for the rest of my life. You are either growing or you're dying. There is no middle ground. Committing yourself to continuous learning is a key to mastering mediocrity.

Experts say you should invest ten percent of your income on continuing education. I agree. In my case, the return on investment is difficult to measure because it is an annuity that will pay me back forever.

In addition, by working on myself, it changed my relationship with Lisa and the kids. My children learned these principles at the same time as us because the tapes were always playing in the car. We literally changed the trajectory of generations. I honestly don't know if we would've stayed married through the many crises I dragged us through without the support system we had subscribed to.

I will always be thankful for the INA educational system. There is one book that every kid graduating college or a person who desires success should read and reread every year. The book is *How to Win Friends and Influence People* by Dale Carnegie. This book changed my life, especially once I realized that my wife is a people too!

CHAPTER 8

DREAM BUILDING, BOLDNESS AND GOALS

I REMEMBER BACK BEFORE I MET LISA MY BEST FRIEND Mike and I attended an all-day seminar on a Saturday. We thought we were going to learn how to be rich but as it turned out it was a seminar on how to "think" rich.

I was so angry. There was so much more I could be doing with my time, like mowing the lawn, but there we were wasting our time learning how to think. I thought I was already goal driven. I wanted to be wealthy and happy. I was already working harder than most people I knew.

The speaker began the gymnastics of helping a bunch people understand the neuroscience and statistics behind the power of positive thinking with many examples and proofs of its effectiveness.

He shared an article from Forbes magazine. It was a remarkable study about goal setting carried out in the Harvard MBA Program. Harvard's graduate students were asked if they had set clear, written goals for their futures, as well as if they had made specific plans to transform their fantasies into realities.

The result of the study was that only 3% of the students had written goals and plans to accomplish them. Thirteen percent had goals in their minds but had not written them anywhere and 84% had no goals at all.

Think for a moment, which group do you belong to? Ten years later, the same group of students were interviewed again, and the conclusion of the study was astonishing.

The 13% of the class who had goals, but did not write them down, earned twice the amount of the 84% who had no goals. The 3% who had written goals were earning, on average, 10 times as much as the other 97% of the class combined.

Over the years I have seen these statistics repackaged many ways, but it's a principle that can't be ignored. The instructor also shared that how you write down these goals is critical to their success. They need to be written in a positive, proactive fashion, as if they have already happened.

You cannot simply write down a goal like I want to lose ten pounds. You have to write "It's May 30th and I weigh 200 pounds. I feel amazing after losing ten pounds" and the more emotion, the better it is. This principle applies to all your goals in every area of your life. A great book to read on well-rounded healthy goal setting is *Success the Glenn Bland Method*.

Experts teach that you should read your goal card multiple times per day but especially right before you go to sleep at night. You are literally building new neuro pathways in your brain. You are reprogramming yourself to be a goal crushing machine. One of my favorite quotes instead of "fake it until you make it" is "speak it into existence." You can literally speak your dreams and goals into existence with one little caveat, you must be willing to do the work!

Be careful what you speak. The same principle holds true for saying negative things out loud. I knew I was going to do the work either way so if this goal-setting thing could give me an edge, I was all for it. There would be so many times in my life that goal-setting and positive visualization would save my bacon.

Goals are often synonymous with dreams, so Lisa and I used a technique called dream building to help turn our goals into reality.

There is a tremendous library of books and information available on the best techniques for dream building. Visualization is a simple technique which can be used in business and in your personal life. It is a great way to teach your kids how to dream and it is one of the most practical ways I learned how to master mediocrity.

In fact, it is something we did with our family. What was it we really wanted from building a business? What is it my kids would love to have because of our family commitment to building this new venture?

We gathered up all the magazines available, sat down as a family and started cutting out pictures of everything we could imagine. We found pictures of toys, cars, boats, homes, vacations, and other fun things, but we didn't want to limit our dreams just to material items.

We found pictures that represented time together as a family. Another had the word "debt" with a red line through it. The most important picture was of a mother who was home with her children.

Then we went through all the pictures we had discovered and narrowed them down to the ones that were most important to us as a family. We pasted all those pictures to a white poster board and attached it to our refrigerator for the world to see. We told our kids that we now had a magic refrigerator because it held all our dreams.

The pictures would stay there forever and as we achieved them, we would replace those images with new ones. I repeated the process in my daily planner with pictures that were personal to me and continued to do so for years.

Twenty years later I came across those planner dividers with my dream pics and I was amazed to see that we had achieved every single one of those dreams. I had a picture of a big, beautiful house in the country, a red Corvette, time with my kids vacationing, and in bold letters a word that said "millionaire."

The most important picture was the one with Lisa home with the kids. She has been a stay at home mother their whole lives, something we are very proud of. I still have the divider I found in my desk drawer and I like to look at it as a reminder of the struggle and the power of a dream!

Eight months would fly by and the guy who recruited me and Mike into the Amway business was now recruiting us into the insurance business. Apparently, we were gluttons for pain. I naively believed that the flexibility of time the insurance business could offer would give more time to build the Amway business and I would have my weekends back with my family.

When I ran the idea past Lisa, she thought I was insane. In retrospect she was absolutely right, which she often is, but apparently, I like to learn things the hard way.

Transamerica was a large credible company and they were offering us a guarantee for the first few months to make sure we could pay our bills. Commission sales seemed exciting to me because there was no cap on how much I could earn.

What I did not think through clearly was no ceiling meant no floor either. I was about to learn some of the hardest life lessons ever. These lessons would bring me to my knees.

When Mike and I approached our boss, Don Baxter, with the news that we would be leaving our great jobs to pursue a career in life insurance, he laughed at us.

He called us the "Gold Dust Twins" and he was sure to publicly berate us. Looking back now, we had it coming. Once again, everybody I ran the news by thought I was stupid, crazy, and irresponsible. But that is how it goes with me.

The more people that tell me I can't do something, the more resolved I am to succeed. People have been doubting me my whole life and I find great pleasure in proving them wrong. Success is the best revenge.

Selling insurance was similar to Amway; make a list of names and pitch the idea to your friends and family. Although it was scary, it was a great way to get started learning and selling.

It did not take very long to run out of friends and family. This is where most people give up and quit. Fear sets in, self-doubt begins to overwhelm them, and they bail out. Quitting is not part of my DNA, plus I had promises to keep. I was lucky enough to sell a few policies to friends and family, but the rubber was about to meet the road.

My manager coached me that in order to keep the momentum going I had better learn to prospect strangers. He told me to get the biggest phone book I could find, practice my script, and start calling as many people as I could.

He insisted I make at least fifty cold calls every day, so I decided to make a hundred. What I lacked in experience I would make up for with effort. After all, selling is just a numbers game and my kids had already gotten used to eating every day. One hundred calls would get me five appointments and five appointments should result in two to three new sales.

It felt like the phone weighed two hundred pounds. Every time I went to pick it up, I had to quickly put it down before I strained my arm. I really struggled with the process. Self-doubt and fear consumed me.

Some days I would make twenty to thirty calls, get bloodied with rejection, then find ways just to look busy. Other days I would put my head down and power through the calls. When I spent time thinking about the results I wanted instead of the results I didn't want, the process became less threatening.

Here was the kicker, a small detail nobody told me about, when my commission check came in it was far less than what I expected. Why? Because I did not realize that the guarantee I was promised was actually an advance against future commissions and Transamerica wanted their money back! I didn't even earn enough money to pay my bills.

These financial highs and lows would continue throughout the first year. Unfortunately, there were more lows than highs and we were falling deeper into debt. The ironic part of this was I was named Transamerica's "Rookie of the Year" in the Sacramento region and had to go to an awards lunch to give a speech and receive a plaque.

I stood there looking dapper in my new suit, thinking to myself, if Lisa and I were almost starving and I'm the rookie of the year, how the heck are the rest of these people surviving? The salt in the wound would be that the cost of the plaque was taken out of my next check!

There I was a year later, not doing much in the Amway business but talking a good game, giving a half-hearted effort to the insurance business, and getting us deeper and deeper in debt.

Mediocre efforts were bringing me mediocre results. I was feeling like a complete loser! Something had to change, or I was going to destroy our lives. I had not yet mastered mediocrity, but I knew I needed to and fast!

I decided to find out what the most successful people in my branch were doing to succeed and emulate them. The challenge is always that nobody wants to tell you because now you become their competition, so I quietly observed.

Some of these guys were buying lists of new homeowners and marketing life insurance as mortgage insurance. From the outside in, their strategy seemed to be working. But they had already saturated the Sacramento market.

I decided to market in Central California, two hours away. My other challenge was that I had no money to pay for the fliers and newspaper distribution costs. Our branch manager had been coaching us newbies to get an open line of credit to cover our expenses, then each month pay it back when our commissions came in.

I saw no other options, so I made the genius move and got a $25,000 second mortgage on our house. I had the fliers and labels printed, gathered our family together, and we would sit together stuffing envelopes all night long.

This was an effective, but expensive strategy. I would mail out the entire list, hope to get some returned reply cards, then at night I would call on the leads. Once I quickly exhausted the leads, it was time for some good old cold calling.

This was far better than cold calling from a phone book. I booked appointments for the following week and made the drive two hours away to beautiful Central California. I started selling a few policies and gained a little more confidence. I was on the road a lot and found myself getting home after my babies were already asleep.

It was getting very lonely, so I thought of another brilliant idea. Radio Shack had Motorola cell phones on sale for $1000. It looked like a military style phone in a large carrying case with a cord that connected the receiver to the pack. If I bought one, I could call my Lisa from the road when I was feeling sorry for myself, and I could say goodnight to my babies. However, I overlooked one tiny detail, cell usage wasn't free.

My first phone bill was $1300, which was more than my mortgage payments! I was surprised Lisa didn't hang me by the phone cord. Somehow, she continued to believe in me, in spite of all my silly decisions. I had learned another valuable lesson; broke people make broke decisions that lead to more broke decisions.

I was trying to improve on my mediocre efforts but still struggled with overcoming the fear that was holding me back from becoming successful. I doubled down on the books, tapes, and committed myself to a plan with my mentors.

I knew selling insurance had to remain my top priority, but I was meeting a lot of people that I could also prospect for our other business. Regardless if it were a phone call or a face to face opportunity, all it would take is ten seconds of boldness to pull the trigger.

By adopting the idea that all that stands between you and your dreams is ten seconds of boldness, you will be able to find the courage to ask that beautiful girl to dance, ask for your well-deserved promotion, make the scary sales calls or even present your business to billionaires!

Fear is a natural emotion, but I have learned that human nature is not necessarily my friend. Learning to feel the fear and press ahead anyway, has been a tremendous character builder for me. I adopted the saying that if some action scares me, it is probably the right thing to pursue.

How many opportunities to learn and grow have you avoided in your life because it would require you to get out of your comfort zone? Lisa said to me once "If you fight for your limitations, you get to keep them." She was so right.

Why let fear and insecurity stand between you and achieving your dreams and goals? In the insurance business I committed to five presentations per week and in Amway I committed to three presentations per week. No exceptions. Consistency would be the key to turning my life around.

This increase in activity was a major leap for me, but I was tired of constantly feeling like a failure. I could not allow myself to take a day off from achieving my daily minimum activity goals, otherwise my old, bad habits would creep back into my life and derail me.

Creating new habits can be one of the most challenging things for all of us. In my case, I had to decide what I was willing to give up in order to make room for new and healthier habits. Something as simple as turning off the TV and reading a book would prove to be life changing. I had to eat, sleep and drink goals until they became my new normal.

So many new things in life seem difficult at first, but after time they feel natural and easy. The people around me probably thought I was obsessed, but I was tired of listening to the negative opinions of people who were trying to hold me back. I would rather seem obsessed with my goals than look like a failure.

It took me about six months to build sustainable momentum. As a result of my consistent efforts, I started making some decent money in the insurance business.

Simultaneously we built up our Amway business to $800 per month in net profits. On the surface, we were getting by, but the gravitational pull of our debt kept dragging us deeper into the hole.

The negative effect of compounding interest on debt was working against us 24 hours a day. We had borrowed money from our parents, leveraged multiple credit cards, and we were upside down on our mortgage.

We were paying every bill late if we were paying them at all. Most of our bills were at least three months behind. It wasn't unusual to have the phone shut off or lose power to the house. It was an incredibly stressful way of living.

Still, Lisa found ways to make it fun for the kids. When the power was shut off, we just pretended we were camping inside the house. Also, when the phone got turned off, the creditors were not able to hound us all night long. They did the next best thing and called our neighbors to see if we still lived in the house. Very embarrassing. There was way more month than money and the creditors were about to come knocking.

This was one of the most frustrating challenges to deal with once I had made the quality decision to change my life. Just because we had decided to change didn't mean we could ignore all the prior mistakes we had already made.

This would prove to be a defining moment in my life. I had the choice to crumble under the weight of my past poor choices or I could dig deep into my soul and decide to man-up and be the leader God created me to be.

We can expect that any time we decide to make a quality change in our lives, that the forces of evil will attempt to drag us back into the pit of despair. Expect it and prepare to do battle. My battle was now here.

CHAPTER 9

ON MY KNEES

IF YOU'RE GOING TO BE BROKE, DRIVE A FAST CAR! Things had become dire around the Flowers' home. I started making some proactively desperate moves and made some deep financial cuts.

I drove my truck back to the Chevy dealership and convinced them to buy it back. We were down to one car so Lisa was stranded at home until I would get back from work. The bigger issue was that our babies needed their well-baby care shots and Lisa had no way to get them to a doctor. What made the situation even worse was that we had no health insurance.

Lisa, being the get it done girl she is, put one baby in a backpack and the other in the baby seat on my old green Schwinn ten-speed bike that I bought back in high school for ten dollars. She peddled them through town to the free clinic for their shots.

When Lisa told me what she did, rather than feeling proud of her for acting like a good mother, I was furious with her for all the wrong reasons. We lived in the town I grew up in and I was more concerned with what people would think of us than the fact that she did what she had to do.

I knew the repo guys would be looking for me since I had not made a car payment on my Mustang in months. At night I was parking my car in Mike's garage so nobody would see it and try to take it. During the day I was keeping my eyes peeled for anything out of the ordinary.

We lived in a circle, so when I came home, it was easy to spot the two repo guys sitting on point in their old Chrysler. I drove around the circle and pulled over on the opposite side of the street a few houses away from where we lived. I could see them coming so I decided to make them chase me. They quickly turned around and I stepped on the gas, but not too fast because I didn't want to lose them just yet.

We lived on the edge of town and I knew all the old country roads. I led them, twisting and turning, about six miles away out near Camp Far West Lake before I decided to leave them in the dust. I floored my gas pedal and left them behind in seconds.

I was confident they were lost so it would buy me enough time to go grab Lisa and the kids and find refuge at her parent's house. This went on for a few days, until they decided to up their game.

Lisa had been coaching the kids that if any stranger came knocking on the door, they were to stop whatever they were doing, drop to the floor, roll to the hallway, and go hide in our bedroom.

That afternoon Lisa spotted two huge, scary looking bruisers coming up the sidewalk. She was frightened by the sight of these guys, but her training kicked in. She whispered loudly, stop, drop, and roll. The kids all did as instructed. My frightened family hid in the bedroom while the beasts pounded on the front door yelling "we know you're in there!"

When I came home, Lisa was still shaken from the experience. I was near my breaking point. All I ever wanted in life was to have my own family, and now I was failing them miserably. In some areas I felt like I was improving but it was too little, too late. The financial hole I dug was too deep.

That night I could not sleep a wink. I laid there feeling like a complete and total failure. I was failing my wife, failing my kids, and failing everyone that had ever believed in me. My self-image was at the lowest point of my life. Tears welled in my eyes and I quietly slipped out of bed, down to my knees.

I prayed to God to help me understand why I seemed to sabotage the good things I attempted to do. I told God that I knew I was built for greatness and I submitted myself to him.

I asked our Lord to guide me and I promised to do whatever it would take to get the work done. "I will do what scares me because I know in my heart, I can do anything." I was crying, but it felt good to release all the negative emotions. "I will be the man I need to be, the leader I need to be, the father and husband I need to become."

I was taken back to a time when I had first started playing baseball. I was nine years old playing on a team coached by a local Baptist minister. He was probably in his early forties, although he looked like an old man to me.

He wore two big, white hearing aids that would occasionally throw off a high frequency buzz that would make all the neighborhood dogs bark. He was a nice man who was there to make sure we had fun and learned a few life lessons.

We were playing a team full of my school classmates. I was pumped up and wanted to show off a little. I was standing on second base when my teammate hit a ball to left field. It was a one hopper that landed right in the outfielder's glove. I was already headed to third base, there was no stopping me now.

Ignoring the signal from my coach to hold up at third, I just kept on going. When I raised my eyes to focus on my goal of home plate, I saw the catcher standing there in all his protective gear, blocking the plate with the ball already in his glove. I was determined to score so nothing was going to stop me. I lowered my shoulder and blasted the catcher with all the force I could muster.

It was a dangerous collision that sent the catcher flying on his back, gasping for air. I found my way to home plate touching it with my dirty cleat. At that exact same moment, my uncle Butch who was umpiring the game snatched me by the shoulder and told me that if I ever did something like that again to embarrass our family, he would personally beat my little butt.

I yanked away from his clutch and made my way to the dugout where my preacher coach was standing, waiting to teach me all about good sportsmanship. Then he rewarded my efforts by benching me for the rest of the game.

I sat there riding the pine, angrily waiting for the game to end. As soon as the game was over, I made my way to my father expecting him jump on the family bandwagon with my uncle Butch. He just looked at me and said nothing, which was far worse than yelling.

During the car ride home, I announced (in my stupidity) that I would be quitting the team. My dad still said nothing. I had enough, I was quitting!

He pulled into the drive and put the car in park. He turned his head, looking at me square in my eyes and said "Let me tell you something right now. Once you commit yourself to something you do not get to quit as soon as things get hard for you. You are representing our family name and the Flowers' aren't quitters. You will finish the season, then, if you decide you're done with baseball forever, you don't have to play anymore, but quitting isn't an option, so you had better figure out a way to make the best of it, and always remember this, once you quit anything, quitting in the future will get easier and easier."

That memory and his powerful words passed through my mind like a flash. He was right, I had to remind myself that the

Flowers' aren't quitters. There was no way I was going to quit now on my career or on my wife and kids. Quitting was not an option. Mediocrity would not defeat me.

I'm not sure how long I stayed on my knees, but it seemed like hours. A calmness came over me. A decision had been made. I had heard it said that God can't steer a parked car, so I had better get moving!

The next day I contacted Ford financing and made arrangements to turn in my only car. Lisa and I scrounged together enough money to buy an old, brown Jeep Wrangler so I could get to work, and because it could hold car seats for the kids.

My poor daughter was barely tall enough to reach the phone, but she was well trained in screening out bill collectors, calls she still remembers as an adult. It was humiliating to use my daughter as a human shield because I was too scared to deal with my problems.

I had to put an end to her acting as my secretary, so I finally contacted everyone we owed money to and let them know that I had every intention to pay them, but they had to be willing to work with me.

Our house was already in foreclosure, but I convinced the mortgage company to give me a little more time and I would make it right.

A few months later, I decided it was crazy to keep throwing money at a house we were so upside-down in. So, I contacted the mortgage company and arranged for a short sale. All of this may seem like losing, but for the first time I was facing reality and proactively taking control of our financial future.

We were a couple hundred thousand dollars in debt, due and payable, but I had tremendous sense of relief. I had no intention of bailing out on my debt. That was not how I was raised, I planned to pay back every penny.

I was representing my family name and I was going to make this right. But In order for me to change my outcome I had to dramatically change how I thought, and I had to get off my knees and pick myself up again

If it is true that we deserve to be where we are today based on the sum total of the decisions we've made, then in order for my future to change it was imperative for me to change how I made decisions.

We make decisions based on our belief system that is fed by our thoughts, so what we think about most will ultimately determine who we are and how we live. Are we hard wired to think the way we do because of the way we grew up or is there a way to change how we think? I was determined to find out the answer to this dilemma.

CHAPTER 10

PICKING YOURSELF UP

I REMEMBER WHEN MY MOTHER-IN-LAW KATHY, ONE OF the most positive and supportive people I have ever known, was preparing for her daughter's funeral. She came across three letters that had been sitting on my father-in-law, Irwin's desk.

She had not been in that room for months and while searching for Julie's birth certificate she noticed three envelopes sitting stacked right in the middle of the desk, in plain sight. For some reason, perhaps a God-wink, they caught her eye.

They were postmarked and dated ten years earlier. Neither she nor Irwin recalled the letters, but there they were already opened, and likely read ten years ago, but forgotten over time.

The first letter was a thank you to her father for funding her trip to Italy. It was a beautiful cruise to the Italian Riviera with her mother, sisters, and nieces. The pictures told a story of beautiful journey with a smiling, happy Julie making great memories with her family.

Reading the letter was a reminder of the Julie we all want to remember. The girl who lit up the room when she entered with her energy and excitement. Julie had a way of making the smallest of moments feel like a celebration.

In the second letter Julie wrote down all her favorite memories up to the age of fifteen. It was so much fun to read. She had pages full of memories that were near and dear to her. I smiled and laughed a little when I read them. She was interesting, loving and a little quirky.

The third letter had a very different tone than the previous two. This letter was an apology Julie wrote to her mother. She explained why she consistently pulled away and hid from the realities of life. Three years prior to writing the third letter, thirteen years ago, Julie went through a divorce.

Although it was a toxic relationship, Julie was committed to be the best mother to her son and daughter she could be. Even though the children were already teenagers, Julie was willing to endure the misery to create the visual that all was good. Julie took the divorce as just another failure and made it her cross to bear for the rest of her life.

She told her mother that she felt like a failure who did not deserve to be loved. "Your other children are so successful, and I have done nothing with my life." Julie went on to say that she would never be loved, did not deserve love, and would always be alone. The letter read as if she wrote it the day before she died, not ten years earlier. It was heartbreaking to read.

Julie was never a drinker. On one of her first dates after her divorce, Julie was reintroduced to alcohol. She found the temporary numbing effects to be a welcomed distraction. Julie had a guy showing interest in her and so she was willing to participate in his negative activities. Julie bragged about how all the alcohol fueled crazy things they were doing and how exhilarating it was.

Soon two drinks weren't enough for her to numb the memories. Ten years later two drinks became half gallons of cheap vodka. The tragic ending to this story is that my beautiful sister-in-law, at the young age of fifty, literally drank herself to death, suicide by bottle.

Sad to say, I already knew how the movie was going to end. It was a remake of my mother's story. Twenty-five years earlier, my mother was lying in a hospital bed just the same as Julie. The doctors were trying to make her as comfortable as possible, as she lay silent and motionless in a drug induced coma. Lisa and I walked into the room as my siblings waited in the hall. We were all there to say our goodbyes.

As I looked at my mother all I could think about wasn't all the terrible things that transpired before this, I could only think of all the memories with my family she would never experience.

Although at the time I was very bitter about the whole situation, I didn't want my mother to pass with the burden of our estranged relationship, so I slowly walked up to her, took her hand in mine, and whispered "I forgive you."

While I thought I was forgiving mother for all her mistakes, I was unknowingly setting myself free from carrying the burden for my broken childhood. I understood I could not control the decisions she made, but I definitely had control to choose how I was going to respond.

Both Julie and my mother were wonderful people and I wish their stories would have turned out differently. I wonder what movies were replaying in their heads over and over that drove them to such sad places. I share these two tragic stories as examples to illustrate the power of thought.

What we choose to invest our time thinking about will eventually manifest into actions. If we continually think about the mediocre, we will become mediocre. These actions are derived from the belief system that guides our lives. It is not the world that determines what we do with our lives. We have complete control.

We live in a time when depression is the number one treated mental disorder and probably one of the most misunderstood illnesses in society. I have a passion for helping returning veterans who come home from war just to kill themselves.

My son-in-law AJ served as a Marine infantryman with two tours in Iraq and has seen and done unspeakable things to survive. He experienced the hell of combat in Fallujah!

AJ returned home with the mental scars of a battle torn warrior. At the time I had no idea what his experiences were, and I showed little grace. After all, when he started dating my beautiful daughter, he was a gold chain wearing wanna' be rapper, muscle bound middle linebacker who in my eyes had bad intentions with my little girl.

Turns out I was right, but today I love and respect him. He turned out to be an amazing husband to my daughter and a fantastic father to my three beautiful granddaughters. I am very proud of him.

When AJ came home, he struggled with normal civilian life as so many combat veterans do. The typical resolution has been a prescription from the VA and misunderstanding civilians expecting these guys to man-up and deal with it. I was as ignorant as most and I will always regret not taking the time to understand what he was going through.

I am incredibly grateful that AJ found a way to deal and heal through peer counseling, a college course on faith, and unconditional love from his wife. With God and Melissa at his side AJ found a way where so many do not.

The suicide rate for veterans is staggering. The public number is twenty-two per day. That number may be high or low. Just one is a heartbreaking number.

Even years after coming home AJ has received calls with the news that another buddy has taken his own life. We try to make sense of the things we do not understand. They all have much to live for. Why would they do this?

Some battle scars are obvious while others we cannot see at all. Suicide, addiction, and depression have a very close and interconnected relationship. More than 90% of people who fall victim to suicide suffer from depression, have a substance abuse disorder, or both.

Experts say that depression, suicide, and addictions are closely related. Suicide is the tenth leading cause of death in America. Regardless if its opioids, alcohol or some other weapon of choice, people are dying all around us and are in desperate need of picking themselves up and getting back on their feet through a support system

Julie's written words described in detail her belief system and her feelings of no self-worth, and low self-esteem that ultimately led to a shattered life and early death. During that same time period Lisa and I learned to how to write goals and positive affirmations that we read many times per day.

We committed to reading books and associated with people who believed in us, uplifted us, and challenged us to be better. Today Lisa is living the life that she always dreamed of. She is an amazing wife, mother, and grandmother. She is a strong, principle driven woman who makes me want to be a better man.

I share this not to compare two sisters against one another or to say look how good we have done. I share this because it is a perfect example of two people who had very similar childhoods, experienced very similar teenage years, making many of the exact same mistakes. These are two people's paths ran parallel for most of their lives, yet their outcomes were so different.

I do believe people are uniquely wired and are born with certain tendencies. I also believe we have the ability to rewire ourselves for success in an effort to overcome mediocrity, if we are willing to pay the price.

Both women wrote down their thoughts, professed their outcomes, and spent the next ten years focused on making it happen. Inch by inch, thought by thought, action by action, the two parallel paths slowly separated with one leading to an amazing life and the other leading to tragedy.

These might be seem like extreme examples, but they are more common than not. The power of your thoughts will make you or they will break you. They can lead you to a life of achieving your dreams and goals or they can lead you to a settle-for, mediocre life where dreams go to die.

CHAPTER 11

LEVERAGING TIME

As it might already be apparent, few things bother me more than people who have victimized themselves and blame mommy and daddy, and everyone else for their problems. Our futures are not predetermined by our past. It is critical we leave all the garbage in the past where it belongs.

Lisa and I certainly have had plenty of learning opportunities and have been very blessed to have people in our lives to encourage and inspire us. Thank God Lisa is a fighter and has been willing to stick by my side even when I didn't deserve it.

Not long after the time spent on my knees, I found a job with an insurance company who paid a solid base with the ability to earn commissions. They were using whole life insurance to fund retirement plans for franchisees. The companies we were authorized to sell to were Southland Corp who owned 7-11 stores, Shell gas stations, Chevron gas stations, and Purina foods.

I was doing well and was their top producer the first two months I was employed. We had concurrently built up our Amway business to where we were making about $1500 per month and we had just qualified for a $10,000 bonus and a trip to San Diego.

I had also asked Don for a weekend job back at Corti Brothers working twenty hours per week so I could make extra cash but also qualify for health benefits. I was working seven days a week, but we were all in this as a family. If mediocrity was going to be mastered, it was going to take time and effort!

We cut up all our credit cards and we were dedicated to paying back all the money we owed. Our goal was 'to get back to broke,' with no debt of any kind. A true start-over, a clean slate.

I just needed some financial dignity. Never again would we finance a car or buy anything on time, with the exception of a house. We would pay cash for everything and master the art of delayed gratification.

I had learned that most people were far past being broke. They may live in a nice house and drive nice cars, but typical Americans are so far in debt with credit cards and financed toys that if they lost their jobs, they could live on their savings for only a short period. In a pinch, they would lose everything.

Many people said we should file for bankruptcy, which may have been a smart financial move, but our family name meant everything to me. There was no way I wanted that blemish on my record.

Plus, why would I take advice from people who were not living the kind of life I intended to live? Look at what the masses are doing and do the opposite. Years later we would all witness the devastation to our economy when the banks crashed and all those people who were living beyond their means, lost their homes and most of what they owned.

Since we decided to walk from our house, I did not want to waste money on rent, so we drove to Lisa's parents and pitched a plan that included living with them for one year. We would take the year to save money while paying down as much debt as we could.

When it was all said and done Lisa and I were hundreds of thousands of dollars in debt, due and payable. Since bankruptcy was not an option for us personally, we had to commit to a plan to get out of debt.

The very first thing we did was cut up all our credit cards and taped them to the bathroom mirror. I would be reminded of our commitment every morning when I was getting ready for work.

Next, we wrote down the payment and balance on every outstanding debt we had at the time. With a little financial counsel we decided the best strategy would be to contact every debtor and let them know we intended to pay but they were all going to need to work with us otherwise we would be forced to default.

Surprisingly, most of them agreed but it required me to be very firm, not negative, but firm. I informed them that I would not stand for any bully tactics or threats otherwise I would cease all communication and they would not be paid at all.

We decided to start with the credit card that had the smallest balance even though it did not have the highest interest rate. The important thing was for us to establish a win by paying off a card completely.

Since there was already more month than money, we had to find the extra funds somewhere. We would track, trim, and apply. We dedicated ourselves to tracking and writing down every penny we spent on everything and it was surprising how much money we were wasting on non-essential items like fast food, snacks, coffee, cable TV, video rentals, eating out, and more. We found a few hundred dollars immediately that we could trim from unnecessary spending and apply that money to the targeted credit card.

We also applied all the money we were trying to make the monthly minimal payments with on the other credit cards to the targeted card. Within just a few months we had paid the card down to zero and closed the account.

We had achieved a milestone victory and it felt great. We then took all the money we were paying on the first card and applied it to the next card with the lowest balance in addition to the additional money we found by continuing to track and trim.

We repeated this process until all our credit cards were paid off. Was it easy? Absolutely not. We had to grind it out for years, but the process changed our approach to debt forever. We will never again be enslaved to a lender. You decide what you're willing to give up in order to get what you do want out of life.

I am forever incredibly grateful for Kathy and Irwin Clark who have always been there when we needed them. They had no hesitation in accepting us into their home, but only if we stayed committed to the plan.

That weekend we packed up a few trucks and made the drive to our new home. When we drove away from our first home that we were so proud of my heart hurt with a sense of failure, but we were desperate for positive change. During the short drive to Newcastle I shifted my thinking from regret to possibilities.

As I pulled into the driveway my mind went back to the time, many years earlier, when I drove into that same driveway looking for my future bride. I'm sure Lisa's parents never expected to have their son-in-law return with three little kids and a soon to be pregnant Lisa.

We had decided that we were going to make sure Lisa's parents weren't too sorry that we invaded their quiet home with our family chaos, so Lisa did most of the cooking and helped with the cleaning. When I had the time, I would help with all the yardwork and assist anywhere I could.

We tried to bring some value to the people who were supporting our change. We were working hard to chip away at our debt and pay for my mistakes, but we had never given up on our dreams.

While living there, not a single time did her parents make us feel unwelcome. Kathy cheered us on, and Irv kept us accountable. Lisa and I were doing pretty well, and we were very proud that we decided to put our egos aside and own up to our mistakes. We were determined to grind our way out of debt.

Our kids would now grow up with parents who preached financial responsibility because we were educated by fire. We knew what we were talking about. We were earning our PhDs in finance the hard way and we were committed to devoting all the time necessary to making things right and getting on the fast track success.

In the process we became all too familiar with a concept that I have lived by since. The concept, which I mentioned previously in passing, is that time will either promote you, or expose you. Does 10,000 hours of activity make you an expert? Yes and no.

As Malcolm Gladwell discussed in his bestseller, *Outliers*, to become an expert at anything it takes ten thousand hours, or approximately ten years, of deliberate practice to become great.

One of the examples Gladwell uses to illustrate this point is the superstar band The Beatles. Before their musical invasion into the U.S. and their rise to super stardom, the band perfected their music playing skills in the St. Pauli quarter of Hamburg Germany, a dangerous area, full of prostitutes and strip clubs. They would play incredibly long sets week after week, for years in this nasty place, but they were perfecting their craft.

We see the finished product of famous musical acts, professional athletes, and wealthy business people, who make it seem that they are naturals at what they do, but what we don't see is the daily grind, year after year, to become the absolute best they can be. We are not there to witness all their struggles, tears, and disappointments. We only get to see the finished product.

We have all heard the statement that practice makes perfect, but the reality is only perfect practice, over long periods of time, makes perfect. Mastering mediocrity takes practice and time.

Considering this we make many excuses. We doubt our abilities and talents by saying and thinking things like "I'm just a normal person" or "I can't sing or dunk a basketball" and things like "nobody in my family has ever been wealthy, I have no obvious talents."

Regrettably, I'm just as guilty as we all are in this regard. I have either said or heard all these excuses and so have you. If you fight for your limitations you get to keep them, and they will own you forever!

I heard a speaker share this statement once and it has always stuck in my mind. He said, "God would never give you a dream without a way to achieve it." Deep in our souls we all believe we can be better than we are, but we live in a world that promotes mediocrity. This is why we are inspired by the incredible stories of people who overcome unsurmountable obstacles to achieve their dreams.

I love watching Rocky movies and have enjoyed all ten of them. Stallone wrote the screenplay for Rocky in three and a half days, right after watching the championship match between Muhammad Ali and Chuck Wepner in 1975.

After forty-five years, Rocky movies are still inspiring people to overcome their own challenges. The Rocky theme song is probably playing in your head right now.

What you lack in talent, you can overcome with heart. Replace complacency with hunger, and self-doubt with desire. These stories resonate with the public because they remind us that we all possess heart, and they stir the hunger and desire inside our souls.

God willing, we all have ten thousand hours in our futures, so what will we do with our time? It is never too late to start learning and growing. Time will either promote your strengths or expose your weaknesses.

The beautiful thing is that you and I have complete control over the outcome. If we don't choose to control our time, by default we allow the world to control it for us. Time is our most precious commodity and once passed we can never get it back. Do not waste time thinking about doing something to improve your life. Act on it now.

Sometimes people will try to overcompensate for mistakes by applying massive effort or decide to make major changes all at once which often results in failure. While living with Lisa's parents, rather than try to make drastic changes, we decided to do something small every day to create forward progress. Over time, these small decisions compounded into dramatically positive change.

It is human nature to start down a path towards exercise, weight loss, improved finances, or any other worthy cause just to become discouraged and quit.

When you are in a deep hole it is extremely difficult to look down the road and sustain effort over long enough periods of time to see the results. We live in a microwave society that tells us we deserve results now. Take the magic weight loss pill, buy the new video to get six pack abs in five minutes, or play the lottery to get rich.

On the surface it appears that the changes we must make, in order to succeed, are so big there is no way we can sustain the effort, so people get discouraged and quit. Quitting has become an acceptable part of today's society.

Nobody wants to read a book titled *The Art of Procrastination and Excuse Making*. I believe most people want to make positive changes in their lives and they just need help understanding the process and the support to achieve their goals. We can achieve huge goals just by starting with small changes that, compounded over time will bring the results we desire.

Time is the great equalizer and if employed correctly you can achieve amazing results in anything you do. It is imperative you identify the most important tasks required for you to succeed and apply consistency without compromise.

You must work on these tasks every single day without fail. Compounded interest cannot work for you if you put money in and take money out. Just like interest compounded, time cannot work for you if you are inconsistent with your activity.

There are two books I have read on this topic that changed my life. First was *The Slight Edge* by Jeff Olson and second was *The Compound Effect* by Darren Hardy. The principles written about by these two authors are very similar.

The small, seemingly insignificant things we do, day in and day out, will compound over time. This is what we refer to as "the grind." The multiplier and essential ingredient is time. Are you grinding your way towards success or are you drifting your way towards failure?

Both action and inaction require time and effort. We have all heard of Newton's law of inertia, an object at rest stays at rest and an object in motion stays in motion with the same speed and in the same direction unless acted upon by an unbalanced force. Get yourself a little out of balance and act now.

Procrastination is just failure on layaway, and it keeps us from mastering mediocrity. We burn so many calories talking about what we should do instead of just doing what needs to be done. Recognize that everything we do will either bring us the results we want or by default we will get what we do not want.

The key to achievement by harnessing the power of the compound effect is consistency. Implement the principles we discussed around goal setting. Commit yourself to the compound effect, and you will achieve your dreams and goals.

Consistency and the compound effect are not just a one-time decision. You will need to make small, supporting decisions every day to achieve the change you want. Small incremental changes result in large dramatic results.

Do I eat the burger and fries, or do I eat the salad? Do I take a long walk, or do I sit around doing nothing? Do I watch TV, or do I listen to this podcast on success? Do I finance this now or do I save the money and pay cash? Do I allow myself to think negative thoughts or do I look for the positive? Do I have a problem, or do I have a challenge? Do I spend time with negative people who drag me down or do I find a circle of friends who encourage me to be better?

These are all decisions you make every day of your life. You are in control. The key is forward motion, every day.

CHAPTER 12

POSITIVE MOMENTUM

YEARS AGO, I LISTENED TO A RECORDING BY JIM FLOOR titled *Momentum is Not a Mystery.* In it Jim explains the nuances around building momentum in business and the application of key principals compounded over time.

One of the statements he made has stuck with me for years. Jim said that momentum is very difficult to build and once you have it, momentum must be carefully nurtured. If you do not pay attention to your KPIs, key performance indicators, you will lose the momentum you created, and once it's lost, it's extremely difficult to ever get back.

Momentum is agnostic, it doesn't care if it is negative or positive. Momentum doesn't care if it's working for you or against you. It can build you up or it can tear you down. It can make you wealthy or it can make you poor.

The great news is that you are in complete control of your personal momentum. In simple terms, I like to call it forward motion. It is very difficult to maintain a high level of focus and effort every single day when life is coming at us from every angle, so rather than do nothing, do something to move yourself forward; even if it's just a small step.

Whatever you do, avoid doing nothing. Nothingness is just a way for mediocrity to master you and it can easily break the good habits you are fighting to maintain. So, lean forward and do something positive that aligns with your goals. Remember that broken focus is the enemy of momentum.

Lisa and I had been living with her parents for a little less than a year when Kathy came to me and asked me if I would be interested in working for a company that my brother-in-law Mark recently acquired.

Mark's parents had started a video rental chain around the Roseville and Sacramento region at the beginning of the video rental boom. Later Mark and his brother would take over the family business and continue to build it on their own.

I always respected Mark and enjoyed spending time with him and Stacey, and I was excited at the prospect of working with him. I called Mark to get the details on the new company.

It was called Northern Video Systems, a distribution company that primarily sold professional video products to videographers, but they also had a one-man video security department where I would be working.

Mark told me that he would be honored if I would join him because if I could sell insurance, I could sell anything. The hilarious part of that is I was terrible at selling insurance, but he still made me feel good.

Then he asked the key question, "How little do you have to make to pay the bills?" Just a few years earlier my total gross income was $18,000 from selling insurance, so anything sounded better than commission sales. Lisa and I definitely learned how to live lean which would become a key practice for us in developing wealth.

Mark and I agreed on a salary of $2500 per month. It wasn't a ton of money to most, but for us it seemed like a dream come true. A few months later Mark and I would walk through the front door of Northern Video at the same time, neither of us had a clue of what to do, but we knew we could figure it out.

During that same time period Lisa and I had built our little home-based business in to a decent sized network earning us a few thousand dollars per month with an annual kicker of ten thousand dollars and trips to Disney World in Orlando, Florida.

I was getting in my ten thousand hours of deliberate practice learning how to prospect strangers out in the wild, doing in-home presentations, and speaking from stage. We had even been invited to speak in front of ten thousand people in a large arena.

We had both committed ourselves to personal and professional growth. Combine personal growth with consistent actions, even though it may be ugly in the beginning, and over time you will see positive changes. We were still working hard to pay off our debt.

It seemed like we got into deep debt over night, but it was taking forever to get out. We were committed, and quitting was never an option! Even though the insurance business had kicked my butt, I still struggled with quitting, but it was time. It was a blessing to have a consistent income that we could budget around.

My first day at Northern Video was in February of 1992. I borrowed my in-laws old Cadillac and drove to Sacramento. I met Mark in the parking lot, and we walked in the door ready to conquer the world. I was introduced to my new coworker Rick Tokunaga. He was the one-man security division.

Rick had worked with Sony Security in the past and was hired by the previous owner to build the security side of the house.

I found Rick to be a little non-social in the beginning. He gave me a brief overview of what he sold and his strategy for gaining new customers, but then made it clear to me I would be own my own.

He handed me some Rolodex cards that contained the names of some manufacturers and instructed me to schedule my own training.

Later Rick and I would become close friends, but in the beginning, he was under the impression that I was hired to take his job, so he was less than friendly. Within a day I had scheduled all my training and I was ready to roll. Rick was taken aback by how positive and excited I was.

Little did he know how grateful I was for this opportunity and I had planned on using it to completely change my life. Lisa and I had created positive momentum and I was committed to never losing it again!

While Rick was working from his Rolodex, I decided to implement a system for prospecting and customer management since we did not have a CRM software system.

Our PCs were used only for order entry and accounting. The system I was taught in the insurance business would work just fine. It was a 3x5 index card file system that was contained in a shoe box. The dividers were marked 1 through 31 representing the days in a month.

The white index card would have the prospect's name, company name, phone number, and any key notes. Every time I would pull a card and call the customer, I would write down the date of the call, any pricing requests and key information regarding their business or their families.

I would then refile the card a week or two later so I could reach out to them again. Once I sold the prospect, I would rewrite the customers information on a gold colored card to separate the prospects from the customers. We used this gold card system for years until we wrote our own "gold card" software CRM.

It is surprising to me how many people suffer from the affliction 'paralysis from analysis.' They don't want to start anything until they have all the details, understand the process, and have a clear plan with identified results. So rather than jump in with both feet, they don't do anything and nothing in their life changes. They just get older and more bitter.

I do understand where they are coming from since I had naively jumped into the insurance business with nothing but faith in my recruiter which was one of the most expensive life lessons I've ever had.

One of my key take-aways from those days was mastering the skill of being a solution-oriented person. I trained myself not to see problems as problems, but as challenges, and challenges always have solutions.

I did not have the luxury of time in order to analyze and plan, I had to get results now! This solutions-first mentality has stayed with me ever since, and it is a critical component to overcoming and mastering mediocrity.

Even though I didn't know anything about selling security, I did know I was selling a tangible product that every security dealer in America had to buy in order to make a living and stay in business.

I knew I could earn a living while learning the technical side of video security. This was relationship selling and my previous years of learning were about to pay off.

I overwhelmed my lack of knowledge with effort. If Rick was making ten calls every day, I would make a hundred. I wrote down my activity goals on a business card and taped it to my desk, right next to my phone.

I knew that sales were just a numbers game, and a high level of activity should reap me a certain amount of sales, and those sales would earn me a certain amount of bonus. Thus, every single call

I would make would ultimately have a dollar value attached to it, regardless if it resulted in a sale or not.

So, for the sake of example, I assigned a five-dollar value to every call, regardless of the results. When I made a hundred call per day the value of that activity would be worth five hundred extra dollars every day.

I was incredibly motivated because I knew every call got me closer to achieving my dreams and goals. I made the law of averages work in my favor.

If you apply a dollar value to every activity you need to do to be financially successful, it will change your approach to managing your time. Are you spending your time or are you investing your time? Those who master mediocrity invest their time.

Every morning, when I walked through the door, I walked straight to my desk and made 10 prospecting calls, before coffee or anything else. Then I made another 90 calls throughout my day to customers I had developed or more new prospects.

A hundred calls would reap me ten packets of introductory information to send out via the U.S. Postal Service. That's right kids, no email yet. Ten info packs would turn into two new customers.

Know your ratios and work the numbers. As your knowledge and skills improve over time so will your ratios. Once your ratios improve, do not back down on your effort and settle for the same results with less effort. Stay committed to your numbers and enjoy greater success.

So, there I was, at a new job that would in hindsight prove to be a major step on my road to mastering mediocrity. Momentum was now on my side but there was still much to learn ahead.

CHAPTER 13

DUPLICATION, ATTITUDE AND INFLUENCE

JOHN D. ROCKEFELLER, ONE OF THE WEALTHIEST MEN in American history, would often say "I would rather earn 1% from 100 people's efforts than 100% of my own efforts."

The only way to earn money beyond our own time, ability, and efforts, other than our spouses working, is to create systems and teach others to duplicate the systems.

If it is true that time is money, then leveraging our time is the key to exponential income growth. If all we do is sell our time for money on a typical job scenario, then our income will max out as soon as we max out our time. How many hours in a day can we work?

In no way am I putting down hourly work, I know plenty of people who make great money working for someone else. The biggest challenge is if something happens to the person who is selling their time for money, the money stops.

My new job at Northern Video saved me because I was motivated to make more money to attack my debt. The best way to make more money in a sales company is to sell more.

I had created a very duplicable system that could easily be taught to others. I could duplicate my time by teaching and training other salespeople resulting in increased sales and more money for my team.

I approached Mark with the idea that I could grow a division of salespeople, with the financial incentive that I would be paid a small percentage of their overall sales. Thankfully, Mark agreed.

I instantly got to work and within a few years we had four productive sales teams resulting in strong revenue growth and a nice increase in everyone's income, including my own.

After a few more years of focused effort, Northern Video, a small unknown company, was becoming one of the largest, privately owned security distributors in America. We were learning, growing, and having fun.

During the same time, in our home-based business, we were experiencing success recruiting and teaching others how to duplicate the system perfected by INA, the business support organization we belonged to. Our personal business had grown to approximately 100 IBOs, independent business owners. We were focused on building large networks of people who used and sold goods and services.

Our core line of products were consumables. These are products used by people every day and when they run out, they buy them again. That means if the IBOs are loyal to buying from their own businesses, they wouldn't have to recreate new sales every month. When they ran out of toilet paper or soap, they would buy it again, and find a few new customers to do the same.

The key to success in that business is building, maintaining, and growing teams of IBOs who use and sell products and plug them into a system of education that promotes personal and professional growth, a system developed by the leaders in INA. All the micro-businesses compounded together added up to a lot of volume, and since we get paid on volume, it was very lucrative.

Every IBO would be encouraged to duplicate the same system making it much easier to teach the newest person to get off the ground, much like a franchise style of business. Learning how to systemize and duplicate became a skill that would pay dividends in every business I owned, up through today.

However, I could have done none of this without the help of others and especially not without a promotable and positive attitude. Develop an attractive personality so other people will be eager to help you succeed. Nobody promotes a mediocre thinker.

Are you the kind of person who brightens up a room when you enter it, or are you the kind of person who brightens up the room when you leave it? Nobody wants to work with negative, sour people who always see the glass half empty. These are the same people who can suck the oxygen right out of a room with their negative, stinking-thinking attitudes.

I will take someone with a positive, can do attitude over another person with a higher aptitude but negative attitude, any day of the week. As a business owner I am looking for people who stand out from the crowd because they have a teachable spirit, desire to grow, and are fun to be around.

How would people describe you when you are not around? Please do not think I believe I'm perfect, because I will be first to admit I have to constantly fight against my nature.

I come across as intense and aloof, and I'm sure there are plenty of people who would add their own superlatives when describing me. I will say though, I've always had a hunger to be different, to be promotable.

Back in my grocery days I figured out what Don and the owners were looking for and I delivered results with a positive, do whatever it takes attitude. Everybody wants to promote a hard-tryer who can follow instructions and get the job done. At Northern

Video it was clear that Mark needed to grow sales for the business to survive, so I grew sales and delivered results.

There is more to being promotable than just effort, there are some other ingredients that are required for the recipe to work, all of which contribute to mastering mediocrity.

Trust is a key ingredient that cannot be overlooked. If your team leader is concerned with what you are doing when nobody is watching, you are probably not promotable. If your efforts are based solely on your emotions, then you are probably not promotable. If you say things like "pay me more and then I will work harder" then you are probably not promotable.

If you always take more than you give, drag people down, you're a gossiper, a victim, lazy and inconsistent, then you're absolutely not promotable. The reality is, we can all be replaced, but we can certainly make it difficult.

One of the keys to my growth in my jobs and my businesses, was I would always put in the effort first, deliver positive results, then ask for compensation commensurate with the results I brought to the table. When you are a promotable person, you will likely always feel under paid for what you do.

Do you make it attractive for people to want to invest time, energy, effort, and money into you? We all need mentors in life, people we can learn from. I am not referring to a manger who is required to train you to perform some job function.

I'm talking about mentors who can share their personal life experiences with you so you can learn the nuances of success. Mentors who can help you to become the best spouse, parent, and human that you can be.

If you are like me, I did not have people knocking down my door trying to tell me how to win in life. I had to execute first, then they appeared over time.

If you are doing whatever it takes to become the best at who you are and what you do, people will be attracted to you and they will want to help you. These people can become tremendous aids in the pursuit of mastery over mediocrity.

If you are building an MLM style business, put out the effort to grow and your upline will be excited to help you. If you are an employee for a company, be the best at what you do, and your employer will be excited to promote you. When you have an idea to start a new business there will be people who will be excited to invest in your new enterprise.

You can become the type of person that others will want to invest themselves in, not just for financial reward, but because they will have a sense of pride for being a part of your journey.

There have been people who have come into my life that have provided me with opportunities for which I will always be grateful. I can honestly say that I did my best to take full advantage of these opportunities to better my life and to create the best future for my family. There have been men and women that Lisa and I have been able to look to as positive examples of how to build a happy, life-long marriage.

As parents we are extremely cautious of who and what we allow to influence our children, but as adults we can easily drop our guard and allow the insidious media and negative people of the world to give us a sense of hopelessness.

I believe John Maxwell has written more books on leadership than any other author I've read. John states that "leadership is influence." I love this simple definition because it makes it clear that ultimately everybody can lead.

Have you ever had anyone tell you to lead by example? If people, by what they say and what they do, are examples to anyone else, then by definition they have influence, good or bad. Are the examples of what you and I do good or are they bad?

We already know that our thoughts determine what we do, so does it not make sense to find examples of people who have a positive influence on how we think? Since nobody is perfect and we all have our faults, then how are we to find the right people to influence us? For me this was a very simple process.

If you always make me feel better about myself for having been around you, if you encourage me to be a better person, a better husband, and a better father, then I will allow you to influence me.

If you are the kind of person that I would want around my kids, then I will let you influence me. If you are willing to respectfully hold me accountable, and you're qualified to do so based on your actions, then I will allow you to influence me. Here are a few examples of people who have been positive influences, and at different times, changed the course of my life.

I have spoken of the love and respect I have for my father because of his willingness to be there for me, my entire life. I have shared examples of Don Baxter's influence on coaching me to become a better man and a quality employee. There are some other people who have been incredibly impactful in ways they may never know, and I would like to share who they are.

I had been working at Northern for a very short period of time when Mark approached me with a fantastic opportunity to buy our own home again. He offered to sell us the home he had grown up in and he was willing to carry the paper himself.

There is absolutely no way we could have qualified for a home loan, so his offer was spectacular. He was also willing to start the payments with an amount we could afford and slightly increase them year over year.

This was a life changing opportunity for us to gain some dignity back and once again have a beautiful place to raise our children. We jumped at the opportunity.

When we informed Lisa's parents of the move, I am sure they were elated, but more importantly we made them proud. While living there we had paid down our debts significantly and had saved an additional $30,000.

Lisa's parents helped us change our lives, and now Mark was helping us change our lives even more. Mastering mediocrity is not just a process, it is a journey and its always lined with people like Mark and Lisa's parents who help you out in unfathomable ways.

During that time, Mark knew that we needed a second car, so he offered to sell me his used Mazda incredibly cheap and allowed me to determine and make whatever monthly payments I wanted. I will be forever grateful for the things Mark did for me and my family in those early years.

We lived in that house for five years before we sold it for double the amount we paid. With that sale we paid off the remainder of all our old debts and we were officially 'back to broke.' In fact, we were debt free with six figures in savings!

When it comes to positive people of influence, the leadership in INA are some of the best examples Lisa and I have on living a life based on sound principles. Wade and Teri Simmons have been mentors to us for decades.

The examples they set for us still influence our lives today. Not only did Wade and Teri teach and help us build a huge Amway business, they taught us how to grow as a couple and as parents. They changed our lives forever, not because of what they said, but because of how they choose to live their lives.

Jim and Margee Floor are two of the most amazing leaders we have ever had the pleasure to know. I have never met a couple who have inspired so many people to become better versions of themselves. They are known worldwide and have changed the lives of thousands of people. They embody strength, character, and grace.

Like Wade and Teri, Jim and Margee are a couple that Lisa and I have tried to emulate the best we could. In addition to the Simmons and Floors, there are so many other leaders in INA that have inspired us to grow. It is our wish that we can pay it forward and inspire current friends and those we have yet to make.

I believe the only way to build long term success is to be a positive influence on other people. It is a life-long commitment to be a positive example for others to follow. We must protect ourselves from the negative influence of people and seek out positive influence from example-based mentors, books, audios, seminars, and associations.

A simple question I ask myself to keep on track is "Would I want my team, my employees or my children doing what I'm doing?" If so, fantastic! If not, make the necessary changes now!

CHAPTER 14

BECOMING AN ENTREPRENEUR

ACCORDING TO WEBSTER ONLINE AN ENTREPRENEUR IS one who organizes, manages, and assumes the risks of a business or enterprise.

I believe that most people have a decent understanding of the word, but do they *really* understand what it means to be an entrepreneur? I have a clear understanding of the definition of infantrymen as well, but unless I have walked in their boots, I *really* do not understand what it means to be an infantryman.

Owning my own business has always appealed to me, even since the days of pushing the lawn mower around the block. I owned a window cleaning business for years and Lisa and I built a home-based business for two decades.

The title of entrepreneur has a very broad meaning and can be assigned to the kid who has a lemonade stand on the corner to Steve Jobs the co-founder of Apple.

I have tremendous respect for all business owners regardless if they are mom and pop shops or Fortune 500 companies. Somebody had a dream and decided to lay it all on the line to pursue it.

After implementing the power of duplication and buying our new home, the stage was set for me to learn what it meant to be an entrepreneur.

I had been working at Northern for ten years and it was clear that I was working to build someone else's dream rather than my own.

I will always be grateful for the opportunities Northern created for me and I believe I had reciprocated by helping build the foundation of a very large and successful company.

I had just finished reading the book *Rich Dad Poor Dad* by Robert Kiyosaki which influenced me to take action on pursuing some of my own dreams. Lisa and I had built our Amway business to a significant size and could live off the profits of that business if we had to, so it afforded me the confidence to take a major risk.

I developed a five-year business plan that I was going to present to Mark that included a promotion for me to VP of Sales and one third ownership of Northern Video.

I presented the plan to Mark with one small caveat. If for any reason the answer was "no," then I would be writing a letter of resignation to pursue a new business idea. Looking back now I appreciate Mark's answer of "no."

Today I understand that it would have been silly for Mark to give up equity in his company. Sitting in his position now, I would respond the same way. The next thing Mark did would change my life forever. Mark didn't get offended by my offer. He responded with a question, "What are your plans?"

I described to Mark the business I wanted to build, and he paid close attention. Over the last few years of working at Northern I had found a niche in Native American gaming and casinos.

There were just a few properties located in Northern California and every property was telling me the same thing. They were sick and tired of these Vegas security integration companies coming into town only when they had a big project and once the project was over, they blew out of town and customer service was non-existent. They felt disrespected and taken advantage of.

The Native American community is very sensitive to disrespect and getting taken advantage of by anyone outside their tribes, and rightfully so.

I had a clear sense of their challenges and believed I had the answer. Every property told me that if I could do all the design and installation, they would give me all their business.

Northern was a distributor and would violate the relationship with their dealer base customers if they were to provide services like that to end-users.

This created the opportunity for me to start an integration company with an emphasis on gaming. Mark and I had a long discussion around what it would take to build the business, including start-up capital and financing.

His next move was very strategic. He told me that he and his brother Paul would love to join me in this new business and would be willing to provide financing by extending terms, allowing me to buy everything SSI needed to sell from Northern Video at a very competitive price. The fantastic thing about his offer was we were able to open the doors of SSI with a very broad product line.

There was only one catch. They would back me only if I were able to go recruit a few key people Northern had lost over the previous few years, the result of a destructive VP who drove away some great talent.

I had planned on calling Rick Tokunaga and Kellie Vogel anyway. They were both key salespeople for me before they left Northern to work with local competitors. I'm not sure if Mark really believed I would ever build a successful business or if he was more concerned that if I ended up working for a competitor, I could cause some havoc.

By backing me he could play damage control by hurting two local competitors and keep me in the fold. Either way, it was a win-win scenario and I planned to take full advantage of this incredible opportunity. Within twenty-four hours I had commitments from both Rick and Kellie.

I wasted no time, the following week we were all in our new office making calls while putting our desks together. I was about to learn what it *really* means to be an entrepreneur. I was beginning to draw a line in the sand between me and mediocrity.

On April 1st, 2002 we launched Surveillance Systems Integration with the dream to become the largest gaming integration company in America.

I wish that were a true statement. My actual goal was to just turn a profit and not lose everything I owned for a second time. I love the quote from Ed Mylett, "Life doesn't happen to you, it happens for you."

Everything that I had been through my entire life had prepared me for this entrepreneurial journey. Every door I knocked on as a kid, every business I approached to clean their windows, the hundreds of people I prospected for the Amway business, the hundreds of in-home presentations I did, the thousands of calls I made trying to sell insurance, the thousands of calls I made selling security, the hundreds of books, tapes, seminars, every failure, every disappointment, losing everything I owned, every trial and tribulation, prepared me to be the leader I needed to be in order to win.

Our plan was to hit the ground running. The team was prepared to call all their contacts to share the news of our new business venture. We were all very excited to be working together again and there was a genuine sense of anticipation as we opened the doors to our new office.

With a sense of pride, I approached the door to unleash SSI's marketing blitzkrieg on our competition. There was only one small challenge. I forgot the key to unlock the building.

This would be the first of a million challenges we were about to face. Remember, we don't have problems, we have challenges. I've had to learn the hard way that bringing emotion into any challenging situation never helps.

I've always had a bit of a chip on my shoulder and some might say I can be a bit reactionary. It has been a very "challenging" bad habit to overcome. A few years back I learned a great technique when looking to solve any problem. There is an underlying principle in every situation.

Clear all the static away and find the principle. Then determine if a principle is being violated or just the practice of that principle. This will provide clarity in assisting you to find a positive solution as you master mediocrity.

As a husband, parent and business owner, high emotions only add unnecessary fuel to the situation and almost always create additional issues. Mastering this one technique has been instrumental, not only with my mental health, but also the mental health of our company and the health of my family.

I continually coach our leaders that they never get to be madder than me. They have all heard me say a million times, "If it's not chemo, it's no big deal."

There is nothing were doing here that is going to be fatal to our business. Take the emotion out of the situation and make a logical decision. Removing the emotion from a discussion allows us to be clear headed and always creates a better environment for solution-oriented conversations.

The other key aspect to creating productive conversation is to always bring solutions when presenting challenges. People who can reduce the emotional element and focus on solutions will be your best employees and can become stronger leaders.

This has been essential when discussing challenges with my kids and especially helpful when discussing challenges with my wife.

On a side note, from a man's perspective, if your wife comes at you with a high level of emotion, the first words out of your mouth probably shouldn't be "hey honey, why don't you take the emotions from the situation before you talk to me and come to me with a solution, not a problem." This will likely backfire.

I have proven this theory to be true. It makes the most sense when dealing with any situation that garners high emotions to take a few minutes to calm down, take a few deep breaths, listen intently, and then shift the focus to solutions.

My experience has been that for this to become part of your culture, it requires consistency from the leader. Your customers will feel the difference and so will your coworkers and family. Mediocrity feeds off of unnecessary emotions, to master it you have to curtail any overly emotional tendencies you may have.

So, there I was, a real entrepreneur. I had already learned so many valuable lessons, but humbly knew I had so many more to learn. You are either growing or you are dying.

Wade once reminded me that if you want more you will have to get better. Now I'm going to really home in on even more specific traits of entrepreneurship and leadership. I want to spend a little time sharing with you what I have learned through the process.

CHAPTER 15

GRIT, RELATIONSHIPS AND SCALE

TO ACHIEVE ANYTHING THAT REQUIRES A LONG PERIOD of activity, it is essential to harness grit in order to grind your way to success. To become the absolute best at anything, to master mediocrity or to build a successful business, it will require long periods of intense focus to master the tedious, seemingly insignificant, building blocks that lead to the ultimate prize. Grit, by definition, is courage, resolve and strength of character. Grind is also dull, hard work.

I have incredible admiration for those people who are the best at what they do, regardless of what it is. Michael Phelps is the most decorated athlete in Olympic history earning twenty-three gold medals.

Most of his races took less than two minutes to complete, and when he won it was usually by a split of a second. Michael started swimming at the age of seven and competed in his first Olympics at age 15. He was still competing in the games at age 28. In his career, he won more medals than 161 countries. He is considered the greatest swimmer of all time.

I love watching that moment when the victor is standing on the podium as the gold medal is draped over his or her head. Their faces glow with pride because they know exactly what was required of them to get there. As the flag is raised and the national anthem begins to play, they recall the lifetime of sacrifices they made.

They remember the thousands of hours of grinding to perfect every movement of their bodies, and the thousands of hours of mental and physical conditioning. We have no idea the sacrifice and pain these Olympians must endure to achieve perfection. We are just there to witness the end, gold medal or not.

Building a business or training to become an elite athlete can be a very lonely experience. I have read stories of CEOs, athletes, actors, and comedians who deal with prolonged periods of depression.

When you are grinding out your ten thousand hours to perfection it is critical you find healthy ways to manage your head space.

I am equally impressed by the struggling single parents who have the grit to do whatever it takes to provide for their children. They are mom, dad, chef, chauffeur, hair stylist, psychologist, relationship expert, teacher, fashion designer, financier, housekeeper, and landscaper.

They are up early and stay up late doing everything they can to create a stable, loving environment so their children can feel loved and secure.

I remember when I was a small boy my father would come home from a long day at his barber shop and cook his famous spaghetti dinner or his hearty meatloaf. I always had a great dinner, clean clothes to wear, and a loving home to live in, but as a child I was completely unaware of the sacrifices he was making for me.

I coached sports for over 20 years. I would see moms and dads rushing to get their kids to practice at the last second. I could see on their faces the wear and tear of being all things to all people.

Often when I would look over to the sideline, I could see them sneaking in a nap or just enjoying a few minutes alone. I have the utmost respect for all parents, single or married, who place the needs of their children before their own.

It is not easy to get up every day and grind away at work or in a business so you can create a great life for your family. Not only is it the right thing to do, it can be one of the most fulfilling things you will ever do.

We are living in the most prosperous times this country has ever seen which has a very dangerous side-effect. When people are not forced to struggle and work, they can develop a sense of entitlement and they are robbed of the opportunity to learn how to grind their way to success.

Some people say that Millennials are lazy and entitled. It may or may not be true, but if it is true, I can't blame them. I give the credit and or blame to their parents. These kids are walking around with mobile technology in their hands that entertains them, provides them with worldwide information, communication, and social media. They don't even have to exert the energy to press buttons because they are equipped with voice command.

In contrast, in order for their parents to complete a book report for school, they had to ride their bicycles to the library for information, and if they were really lucky, their family owned a set of encyclopedias for them to use for information gathering.

Perhaps these Millennials lack self-discipline because everything comes so fast and easy or perhaps, we just don't understand the world they live in and what motivates them? I'm leaning towards a lack of understanding of what motivates them.

I believe humans are built for achievement and that includes millennials as well. Every generation has suffered from an ignorance of what drives the younger generations. I have witnessed this in my own family.

Kids put in hundreds of hours competing in video games. By the time they are in their early twenties some of these kids have put in their 10,000 hours to mastery. There are multiple colleges that actually offer scholarships for gamers.

In 2019 there were eight professional gamers who earned over $10 million dollars. The top earner was the "Ninja" Tyler Blevins who earned $17 million dollars. Tyler did not become the highest paid gamer in America overnight, he had to put in thousands of hours of practice just to be competitive and tens of thousands to become the best.

Does this mean I agree with kids sitting on their bottoms closed up in their bedrooms all day long? Absolutely not. My point is they live in a world I just do not understand. People are getting wealthy by becoming influence marketers on YouTube and Instagram, I have little knowledge on how they do it, but it is happening anyway.

Arnold Schwarzenegger did not become a world-famous body builder by hitting the gym once in a while, it was his life. His body building victories included five Mr. Universe wins, and seven Mr. Olympia wins, which eventually led him to Hollywood and politics.

Gyms are full of people in January who set New Year's resolutions and by March most of them are gone. People come in on Monday, get a little sore, and do not come back until Thursday just to get sore again.

Their bodies never get a chance to adjust to this new strain its getting put through because of their inconsistency and unwillingness to work through the soreness. A couple of protein shakes later, they just quit and go back to dying.

What is it you're not doing every day on your job or in your business that would ultimately lead you to greater successes? Are you taking full responsibility for your success or are you relying on other people to get the work done for you?

I implore you to identify those things that you must do every day to win. Write them down on an index card and commit yourself to irreducible minimums to master mediocrity

A simple example is you know that you need to make 50 calls per day to obtain average results. Instead set a goal to make 100 calls per day with an irreducible minimum of 75, no matter what.

Do this for every action required for you to achieve your dreams and goals and apply consistent time for a year, then measure your results. Do not try to measure your results daily or quarterly, you have got to give it some time to work.

It is demotivating to set a goal to lose weight and then step on the scale the next day just to see you gained a pound. Apply consistency over time and allow the compound effect to work in your favor maintaining grit all the way.

In today's hi-tech world, leveraging technology is the most common and cost-effective way to introduce the launch of your new enterprise. Social media and other electronic platforms have been proven to be effective tools for advertising your business and creating commerce. It can also be a crutch that can result in failure.

When we launched SSI there was no social media or any of the other common tools used by today's young entrepreneurs. We had to rely on old school methods for spreading the word that SSI was open for business.

I decided I would repeat the recipe that had worked in the past by making a list of names and working the list. Each of us would make fifty to a hundred calls every day, an effective method that still works for us eighteen years later.

It is nearly impossible to build any kind of personal relationship using electronic tools. Relationship selling is an art and those who master the art will always out earn those who rely on just attracting web traffic in service-related industries.

In our area of Northern California there are multiple strip malls and shopping centers packed full of retail shops, eateries, and other small businesses. Those businesses rely on advertising and foot traffic to drive sales.

They open the doors with the clock ticking on overhead, praying that somebody will walk through the front door and actually buy something.

I have seen many businesses eventually close the doors only to be replaced by another. Each time, I always think to myself, "How many widgets do they have to sell just to pay the bills?"

Some person put their dreams and goals on the line only to fail. It is a very sad thing to see. They likely closed the doors and walked away riddled with debt.

I decided from day one that we would never become that company. We were going to proactively market to key decision makers who were in positions to make a purchase. We made hundreds of calls every single day. At our peak, we were making a thousand calls per day. It is the same principle as compounding interest.

Just 500 calls per day, multiplied by 50 work weeks equals 125,000 calls per year! Compare that to a small business opening their doors in a strip mall. I highly doubt any of them will ever see 125,000 people walk through their front doors!

This blitzkrieg approach to marketing put us in a position of control rather than praying somebody would walk through the front door to buy something. No other integrators in our industry were doing what we were doing, the way we were doing it.

From the beginning we started creating our competitive advantage. We were developing and perfecting this simple system for success that could easily be duplicated by new sales associates. Anyone who has the desire can learn a script and make a phone call.

That first year was an amazing display of the quality of people I am blessed to have in my life. I had friends and family volunteering to come work for free to help us get off the ground. I even had my mother-in-law, Kathy in there making calls. It was all about relationships both internally and forging them externally through the blitzkrieg of calls that helped us get off to a great start.

Our system allowed us to scale with people who had no previous sales experience. We could keep wages low and newbies could earn as they learned. We had people working for us that started with no industry experience earning minimum wage and today they earn six-digit incomes.

Create systems that help teach and train your future superstars. We also matched up the inside sales team with outside business development managers. Phone calls are fantastic, but combined with face to face meetings, it is a hard combo to beat.

Our goal was to call and knock on the door of every casino in the country until SSI was so ingrained in their minds that when they think of security, they think of SSI.

In the first few years of business, since nobody had ever heard of us, we would spend half our time explaining who we were, what we could do, and where we were located. I know this is standard for all new start-ups, but those were some tough years. We decided our best approach would be to shock and awe them.

We pleaded with them to just give us a chance to quote anything, and when they did, we would shock them with a very low price to get their attention. It would give us an idea at what price level they had been buying at, then we would adjust margins on all other items.

Once we got the chance to quote them, then we would awe them with the best possible customer experience. Again, grit and relationships made this possible.

Customer acquisition should be the number one priority for any business that is going to rely on sales to grow. Scale is key, and it just so happens to stand in direct opposition to mediocrity.

I was blessed to have recruited some of my old team back because in addition to their industry knowledge, they brought a few key accounts with them. We were selling the first day we opened the doors which allowed for a little breathing room as we were getting our feet under us.

We started prospecting for new customers the day we opened. I wish I could say that we targeted our key vertical, but the reality was we were willing to sell to anyone, anything we could.

There were a few of us who focused primarily on gaming, while others had an interesting mix of large retail, commercial and government accounts. We started every day with what I call the ten by nine. This is a metric we tracked closely, daily.

Every single salesperson was, and is, required to make ten prospecting calls to non-customers the first hour of their day. The compound effect of consistently prospecting, day in and day out, would become our secret weapon for growth. By building a broad width of customers, it would prevent the big peaks and valleys of a typical sales organization and help us scale in the process.

We realized early on that there are many more advanced customers who can self-install basic security equipment and accessory items. We could easily sell these items and drop ship directly from the manufacturer to the end-user.

We created a sale without the requirement of stocking inventory. We developed a transactional style business that required very little capital but resulted in great cash flow and is very complimentary to our installation business. We were the only integrator in the country that took such an aggressive approach to product sales.

I wish I could say it was a genius strategy from our inception, but the reality was that all our salespeople had a background in distribution, so we just did what we already knew to do.

Product sales would eventually lead to projects and projects would lead to ongoing product sales. The real genius was and still is product sales keeps us continually engaged with the customer so we could then drive depth and scale.

Let me explain my interpretation of customer depth. You can only drive depth as you gain trust from the customer. Perhaps in the beginning all we sold the customer was a camera. We were the lowest price, so we were awarded the order. As the relationship grows, we continually promote all the other related products we sell.

Now we just aren't getting the camera, we are getting the cable, mounting hardware recording system, the network and eventually the labor to install it.

We apply our in-house principle of providing the best possible customer experience, so we do it faster and better than all the competition. On every single order!

Then, over time as our relationships grow stronger, customers trust us to consult on what manufacturers and products will best fit their needs. This allows us to drive business with our most trusted manufacturer partners who will protect our business and help us improve margins.

This strategy is unique to SSI and those who have attempted to copy us have failed. We have remained committed to continually improving our systems to prevent us from losing sight of what has made us special from the beginning.

A wide customer base that has depth and scale provides financial security. I have had salespeople who relied too heavily on a single customer for most of their income which is incredibly risky. If anything happens to that customer, there will be a very negative impact on their income.

The same issue holds true for companies who rely too heavily on a narrow customer base. Not only are they relying too heavily on all their sales coming from a few customers, but they can also experience cash flow problems if these customers slow pay, or do not pay at all.

CHAPTER 16
GOING NEXT LEVEL

AFTER A YEAR OF BANGING THE PHONES IT BECAME VERY clear to me that to gain any credibility in the gaming vertical, we would need to establish ourselves in Las Vegas.

I booked a flight for the following week and jumped on a plane with Kyle who had agreed to move to Vegas to open our new branch office.

We knew Kyle because we were close friends with his parents Bill and Sue Makimoto who we had met in the Amway business. I had confidence that Kyle came from good stock and that he would do a great job.

The day we landed I found our new Vegas location and somehow, we even found a place for Kyle to live. It is amazing that when you make a quality decision and take action how quickly great things can happen.

Indecisive people can waste so much time analyzing options in fear of making a mistake, but in reality, the bigger mistake is time decay and the result is mediocrity

I did not want to send Kyle to Vegas alone, so we convinced our kids' martial arts instructor Rick Phan to join him on this journey. Rick had come to me months earlier and asked if he could work part time, for free, so he could learn about our business. This spoke volumes about Rick's character. Eighteen years later Rick has never wavered in his commitments.

I knew that Rick and Kyle working together would make Vegas a winner for SSI. The boys loaded up their cars with everything they could carry. I loaded up our brand-new SSI van with tools and equipment. We left town at zero dark thirty and drove nine hours straight through to Las Vegas.

I remember cresting the hill on I-15 and as the Vegas skyline came into view. I felt incredibly excited about what the future of SSI could be.

We hit the ground running doing everything we could to let Vegas know that we were there and ready to work! Soon after opening the Vegas office we were joined by Ruben Gamboa who ran our Vegas installations. All three men are still working with us today and have all developed into very talented team members.

Vegas was a good old boy community. We knew it was going to be very challenging to break into those long-term relationships our competitors had already established, but for SSI, failure was (and still is) never an option. I made follow up trips every month for years. I slept on the boy's couch and we ate fast food to keep costs down. We were paying our price for victory and it was fun.

Opening Vegas was a milestone for SSI. We could now say that we had an HQ in Rocklin and a branch office in Vegas.

Even though in the beginning it was a bit of smoke and mirrors, the Vegas location greatly improved our credibility. At the time it was not the smartest financial move, but it was a strategic win. We put all our chips on the table. We were all in.

My future, and the futures of my family and employees depended on our willingness to burn the ships in the harbor leaving us no way to retreat.

I wanted to create a culture where winning is the only option, so it was, and still is, imperative that I leave my chips on the table, building for longevity. We are in it to win it, together! In the quest to master mediocrity the strategy is the same, go for the win!

One of the biggest mistakes I see entrepreneurs make is taking too much money out of their business to buy a lifestyle they have yet to earn. This leaves their businesses too weak to withstand any financial downturns.

It also leaves them too weak to take advantage of opportunities to grow. It took me going broke to learn the principle of delayed gratification, but it was worth it. Regardless if you are an employee or business owner, stay lean. Live below your means and save all your extra money to build a war chest.

As the CEO, keep your personal wages low and build for profitability. My personal earnings come from company profits. The power in this personal compensation strategy is that it promotes delayed gratification and encourages an environment of making long term, profitable decisions.

Lisa and I had learned to live lean when we were poor and remained committed as we continued to increase our income. We only drove cars that we could pay cash for and never financed vacations on credit cards.

We lived well within our means and began to save money. Remaining debt free was our number one priority for our family and we applied this same principal to building SSI.

Staying lean and building cash reserves allowed SSI to survive the economic crash of 2008. In six years, SSI had grown to $21 million in annual revenue, but the recession drove us backwards. We were lacking laser focus. Yet, desperate times create opportunities for change.

We knew how to sell a ton of products, but I was insecure when it came to the installation and integration side of our company. I was too reliant on leaders who had their own ideas on how to grow the installation side of our company.

These guys had a technical engineering background and were fantastic at installation, but they were poor leaders and weak at building teams.

Rather than get the best out of less people, they preferred the high body count method. They wanted more buildings, more trucks, more installers with a focus on building smaller regional locations.

The problem with that style of brick and mortar business is that it would drive fixed expenses through the roof. We would also be competing with massive companies like ADT.

It was a strategy that worked well in the past with smaller dealers whose primary business was alarm installation and alarm monitoring with an emphasis on building recurring monthly revenue.

However, that was not the style of business I wanted to build. I saw a future in building large, very technical systems. I wanted to become the largest gaming integration company in America, but because of my insecurities, I allowed myself to take advice from people who did not share the same vision.

When the real impact of the economic crash hit us in 2009 it forced me to make some very difficult, but critical decisions. Would I listen to my gut instincts or would I continue to listen to people that I did not agree with?

I had come a long way towards mastering mediocrity, but I had to decide exactly what I wanted our company to look like and what I was going to need to do to get there. I had to decide who would back me 100% and who I would have to cut from the team.

We are a sales company first, so I leaned on who got us there in the first place, my sales team along with some very loyal and talented installers.

SSI had morphed into a company that was over staffed with engineers who thought they were the smartest people in the company.

They went so far that they asked for a sealed off room away from everyone. They even requested salespeople make an appointment in order to gain their counsel. They wanted salespeople to be stripped of decision making. They treated them like they were stupid.

We had built the company in an open environment that allowed for real time communication. We never had divisional silos that breakdown communication. Titles, like hood ornaments, had never determined a person's worth.

We were a strong team and I was not about to allow a bunch of engineers to determine the fate of our company. It was time to make some cuts.

During that time, I read two books that had a significant impact on my decision making. The first was *Good to Great* by Jim Collins and the other was *Steve Jobs* by Walter Isaacson.

A couple of my take-aways from *Good to Great* were, make a distinctive impact and lasting endurance, and from *Steve Jobs* it was all about customer experience.

These ideas made a significant influence on my decision making and helped mold and create our new mission statement: *Create value and establish loyalty by demonstrating distinctive competencies and the best possible customer experience.* The stage was set for a new era.

CHAPTER 17

DISTINCTIVE IMPACT

WHAT ARE THE DIFFERENTIATORS THAT MAKE YOU AND your business unique from your competition? These are important to define as they are critical to mastering mediocrity.

My business integrates security products from different manufacturers together to solve problems for our customers. Guess what? That is exactly what my competition does as well, so what do we do to stand out from the rest?

It started with me and the culture we created internally at SSI. We were already outperforming the competition when it came to response times and quality of work.

I knew it was going to require much more than just performance to dominate, it was going to require belief. It was and remains imperative that my team believes in me and the vision I have for them and for SSI.

Was my vision crystal clear the day we opened the doors? Absolutely not. In the beginning it was all about survival, but over time, with intense focus, we were able to develop a clear destination for SSI.

Where I got stuck was attempting to develop a clear lifetime vision. In reality, we just needed a five-year vision that could be massaged over time. This simple change simplified the process for me.

The key to the effectiveness of our vision was consistency of the message. Our team did not hear a new message every week. They heard the same message week in and week out until they could repeat it themselves. We repeated the process with our mission statement and anything else I wanted to acculturate.

Many new entrepreneurs start businesses with a desire for a better life, to be the person in charge, and to have control over their futures, but they lack clarity.

The same holds true for many people in their personal lives. Do you know exactly what you want your business or your personal life to look like, or are you just hoping for a better future?

Big dreams and a clear vision are symbiotic and need each other to survive. Together with action, they can make life incredibly exciting when you define your future and invest time dwelling on the possibilities.

Your energy levels are at their highest when you are pursuing something you want so bad that you can literally see it, taste it, and feel it.

Some of my best ideas have come when I was in a crisis situation that created a sense of desperation. Others have come to me when my mind was clear and in a peaceful state.

Do whatever you need to do to fulfill your needs at the time, but either way create a vision for yourself that is detailed and crystal clear. I learned the value of a clear vision decades ago that came from a state of desperation.

I learned the value of a clear vision many years ago when Lisa and I had established a family goal to achieve a milestone in our home-based business that would have a very positive financial impact on our family. It included an all-expense paid trip to Disney World and a check for $10,000.

We had been fighting and struggling to claw our way out of debt for years and family vacations had been non-existent. To qualify for this trip, we had to achieve some very strong volume numbers for all twelve months of the calendar year, hence the name of the reward was called "Q12."

This meant I would need to double down on my efforts. This would require me to be out of the house in the evenings three to five nights, every week, for a year. I was already missing my kids and more time out of the house was going to be painful.

On occasion Michael and Austin would push their huge toy box down the hall from their bedroom and use it to block the front door in attempt to prevent me from leaving the house. They would plead and cry, it was heart wrenching.

I desperately needed my entire family to support this new cause. The same holds true for business owners as we ask our teams to join us in pursuit of our company visions.

I sat my entire family down and shared in detail what the sacrifice was for, and more importantly, what was in it for them. This is how to get total buy in from family or employees.

The next part was key. Once we had the group meeting announcing the vision and mission, I followed up every day for the next 365 days, never missing!

Every night before I left the house, I sat with the kids and described in detail the entire trip. I started with waking up in the morning when it was still dark to go to the airport. What they would see and do while we were flying. I described the excitement we would feel when we would see the hotel for the first time.

In vivid detail I spoke of the sweetness of the ice cream we would eat, breakfast with the Disney characters, and of course everything we would do once we hit the park. This dream-building tale would take me at least forty-five minutes to share. I never missed a day, for the entire year.

On a side note, I did include a very important detail that may seem silly to you, but it was very important to me. I talked about how we were going to eat and drink anything we wanted out of the mini fridge. Candy, soda, juice, whatever we wanted.

In the past, Lisa would get furious if I wanted a soda from the mini bar because it cost a few dollars. Instead, we would leave the hotel, walk to a convenience store, and buy a six pack for far less. Put some ice in the bucket and we were good to go.

Of course, because we were broke, she was right. It is what it represented to me that I hated. I had placed us in such a poor financial position that we had to fight over the cost of a stupid soda.

The mini bar represented a victory to me that I desperately needed. The first thing we did when we entered the hotel room was raid the mini bar, and the best part, Lisa didn't say anything!

I had created a vision that was so clear, we all could feel it and taste it as if we were re-living it every day. It was like a memory that had not happened yet. We were internalizing the dream and it was exciting.

People can't get behind us if we are not clear about where we are headed and what's in it for them. The power in this exercise is by professing your goals, dreams and visions out loud, to as many people as you can, you will be more creative and work harder than you would if you kept it to yourself. Mediocrity thrives in isolation, success is born among others.

Unless I wanted to be a complete loser, there was no way I was about to break my kids' hearts by failing. I was hung by the tongue and willing to die before I was willing to quit.

This is a tool I still use today. I challenge you to try it on for size. If it is not your nature, do it anyway. If you are concerned the people around you may think you have gone bananas, do it anyway. It is OK to be different when normal is not working.

I have met many people who are just drifting through life accepting mediocrity as a lifestyle. When you ask them how they are doing, you will hear responses like "another day, another dollar", or "I'm fair to middlin." My all-time favorite is "I'm still above ground."

What a sad way to choose to live. When you stop dreaming or lose sight of where you are headed, negativity always fills the void. I would rather people think I have gone crazy with all the positive talk, versus becoming a person who just drags down other people so I can feel better about myself. Misery loves company!

I brought this same mindset into our office. I once more applied my tried and true "speak it into existence" strategy.

Just like sharing the vision of Disney World with my kids, I shared in detail my vision for the company and how achieving our vision would have a positive impact on all our lives.

Every year we spend time talking about goals and the kind of lives we all want to live. We help our team set emotional goals for their personal lives that we can work towards together.

We have been blessed to see many employees get out of debt, buy their first homes, start families, and invest in their futures. It is incredibly gratifying to be a part of their successes both personally and professionally.

It is my mission to provide the best possible employee experience, so they can in turn provide the best possible customer experience. This all ties into distinctive impact.

I believe we can excel and have fun doing it. We spend more time in the office around the people we work with than we do with our families, so why not make it enjoyable?

Celebrate victories, not just your own; celebrate everyone's victories. When one person wins, we all win! We do something that may seem silly, but it is effective.

When a salesperson lands a new customer or earns an order over $10,000 the salesperson rings a bell that hangs on the wall in the middle of the sales floor. Then they put their business card in a drawing box for a chance to win a $100 gift card at the end of the month.

Just like Pavlov's Law, when that bell rings, the energy level in the room dramatically increases and serves as a reminder that we are winning. We are always looking for ways to reward our people for exceptional work. Here is another one of my personal favorites.

We hired a young family man, Adam Myhre, who had previously worked for a competitor. His former employer had to close the doors. The company had failed. Adam had been required to travel to job sites where he was away from home for months at a time. He is the kind of man who gets teary-eyed when talking about the love he has for his wife and girls.

When I hired him, I promised him that he would not be required to travel like that, and we would make sure he got home weekly to be with his family.

Business was exploding, and against my word, he was traveling like crazy. I never heard him complain. He told me that me that he understood, and he would do whatever it took to help SSI win. I love a hard tryer.

This went on for over a year, and I knew we were stretching him hard. During a phone conversation he asked if he could take a week off to spend time with his family. He wasn't going to take them anywhere on vacation, he just wanted to be with them.

I asked Adam if he could take his girls on vacation where would they love to go if money was not an inhibitor. He told me that he would love to take them to Disney World. That dream pulled at my heart strings.

I shared with him some of my favorite memories of all the Disney trips Lisa and I were blessed to go on with our kids. I told Adam I would give him the week off but only on one condition, he had to take his girls to Disney World, and I was going to pay for it.

He was speechless and with his voice breaking from emotion, all he could say is "Really, are you serious?" I reaffirmed that I was.

I gave him an additional condition. He had to send me some pictures of him and his family making memories at the Magic Kingdom. He was incredibly gracious. When he was thanking me, I could hear his tears through the phone.

Five years later Adam has risen through the ranks and now leads a key division within our company. He has proven to be a great leader and he is one of my favorite people. He and others like him are the true differentiators of SSI. Together, they form an unbeatable team.

Help people change their lives and you can build your own unstoppable team. When you let your impact be distinct then mediocrity will run for the hills.

CHAPTER 18

DRIVE AND ENDURANCE

THE DOT.COM BOOM OF THE 90S CREATED OVERNIGHT millionaires, but it also nurtured a false sense of reality when it comes to what is required to build a solid, profitable business.

Occasionally I hear stories of companies that are acquired for millions within their first few years of business. It is much more likely that entrepreneurs will need to remain motivated for a long period of time.

This long-term motivation is the anthesis to mediocrity. Where mediocrity is content with clocking out early and calling it quits, you have to be able and willing to endure through the good and bad times. There are so many variables we can't control that can possibly interrupt our flow or kill momentum altogether.

The economic crisis in 2008 is a great example of an unpredictable variable. Entrepreneurs understand that outside threats are coming, but some leaders are not mentally prepared to endure the pain.

It is easy to stay motivated when everything is going great, but it is much more difficult to stay motivated when you're getting hammered with challenges. Attitude is everything, however I believe drive and endurance must come from a much deeper place in your soul, possibly even a dark place.

I'm lucky to associate with some very successful entrepreneurs in an organization called Entrepreneurs Organization (EO). In preparing for this book I asked many of my fellow members where their internal drives originate from.

I wanted to know if they sprung from dark places or a happy places. Every one of them had to pause in order to reflect on the question before answering. Many times, you are either running from something, towards something, or a little of both. Ask yourself this question: "Where does my drive come from?"

Do not confuse motivation with drive. Motivation is a fleeting emotion that is not sustainable for long periods of time. Motivation may move you to make a decision, but it will require drive to succeed at anything long term. There are many motivated people that are mediocre but the same is not often the case with those with drive.

Most of the entrepreneurs I asked said that it was about an 80/20 split. 80% of their drive comes from a darker place, while 20% comes from the pursuit of happiness. For me personally, the 80/20 rule applies as well.

I've always had the desire for the nicer things life has to offer; big house, nice cars, fun vacations, same stuff as most people, but those thing have never inspired me to really put my head down and work through the struggles of business.

In my case I tap into the dark side. The part of my soul that remembers being the kid people felt sorry for. The one who has always had to try incredibly hard to be better than mediocre.

I was, for a few years, the man whose lifelong dream was to have my own family to love and support but in reality I was also the man who had failed them.

I'm the guy who had always felt like I had something to prove to the doubters and to the people who thought I would quit. What these people failed to realize is that I would rather die than quit and would do anything to prove them wrong. I'm more driven when I'm intense and angry versus happy. Intensity and anger seem to last much longer.

Does that mean it is all scorched earth with me? Absolutely not. For all of us "intense" type personalities out there, the rest of the world doesn't need to feel uneasy when they are around us.

Keep that stuff inside for you only. Use it as your fuel for keeping your drive alive. Put a smile on your face and refer back to *How to Win Friends and Influence People* so you don't leave a negative wake behind you.

People skills combined with quiet intensity is a winning combination that will attract other winners to you. I admire and respect those of you who are driven by the pursuit of the happier things in life and the rest of us need you for balance in the world.

I'm no expert, but it seems as though many people who call on the darker side had to survive through very difficult childhoods. I've have had friends share stories of abuse, divorce, alcoholism, racism, poverty, death, loneliness, bullies, and this list goes on. Perhaps you too had to endure some incredibly horrible events as a child that left deep scars on your soul?

Like everyone else, you have a choice to make. Do you use these terrible memories to drive you forward to be the best version of yourself, or do you use them as an excuse to be the worst version, or even a *mediocre* version of yourself?

You and I were not born with a silver spoon, we had a plastic spork that we were forced to use to dig out and escape from the prison of our past.

I believe that people who struggled as children have an advantage over those who have had everything handed to them. Kids who come from wealth or fame are forced to work even harder to learn life survival skills.

As a child I would envy those kids who seemed to have it all. Looking back now I would not trade places with them. I'm not suggesting that kids who come from wealth or fame can't rise up to be their best, I'm suggesting that they may be at a disadvantage in contrast to those who have had to fight their way out. Rich or poor, everyone has their own personal struggles to work through.

One idea we might all be able to agree on is that success is the best revenge. Not in a boastful, prideful way, but in the sense that you did the work, you deserve the prize.

There are no participation trophies in entrepreneurship, just winners and losers. If for some reason you fail, learn from your experience, dig deep, and start over. You can't stop a quitter from quitting, and you can't stop a winner from winning.

Our character will not be measured by how many times we are knocked down, just on how many times we are willing to get back up.

This is what I call upon for lasting endurance or being in it for the long haul. If it is different for you, then that is wonderful. Find what works and prepare yourself for the marathon.

From the day I launched my company I have been in a war of attrition with my competitors and have understood that it will take more than drive and grit to outlast them. As the newcomer to the gaming industry we had to be better in every way in order to grab market share. In addition, we needed to be good stewards and wise with our money.

Looking back at 2008, the economic crash provided me the opportunity to re-define what I wanted our company to look like. It also financially crushed one of my key competitors who had taken unnecessary risks and over-extended himself.

Witnessing his demise, I became more resolute than ever that we would become cash flow positive and remain debt free. This decision required me to make long term decisions with the financial health of the company as my leading priority.

Right before the market crashed a dominant gaming integration company who was our biggest competitor at the time, sold to private equity.

This competitor and its founders were a class act and I had hoped one day to be just like them. They dominated the Vegas strip and were always awarded premier projects. They had become the largest gaming integration company in America and were crushing the competition.

During that time, SSI was quickly building momentum living off their scraps while beating smaller regional integrators. Little did I know that the sale of that company to private equity was going to provide us with the opportunity to compete at a higher level.

It is no secret that when a private equity group purchases any company, it is for the sole purpose to sell it for a profit a few years later. It is a short-term investment.

When you are required to boost profits quickly, you are forced to make short term decisions which is rarely in the best interest of the employee or the customer. When you put profits before people it does not take long for the secret sauce of the founders to disappear. Like I often say, time will either promote you or expose you.

SSI continued to focus on providing the best possible customer experience with distinctive impact which creates an upward trajectory while my competition focused on driving short-term profits.

Short term decision making can sometimes have a negative effect on culture which creates a downward trajectory. When a company, or a family, have internal culture issues, outsiders can begin to feel it as well. This is just my opinion and I don't know exactly what took place at this company, only time will tell.

I believe everything I need to know to win lives in the heads of our customers. We have always taken a different approach to customer service. SSI treats every customer like they are the most important because they are.

Regardless if it is a $10 order or $100,000 order, we treat the customer with the same priority. When competitors disappoint their customers and we get the chance to provide a quote or order, we dazzle them with our positive, do whatever it takes customer experience which always keeps our momentum on an upward tick.

When I decided to no longer be held hostage by our previously employed engineering team, I leaned into my sales staff and field services team to replace them.

I was told point blank that we would fail, that salespeople could never design projects of that magnitude. Of course, I shared this insult with our sales team and together we did what I love to do, prove the doubters wrong!

Our team came together and designed a comprehensive job building calculator that we would use to effectively build projects based on questions answered from pre-bid job walks.

With each new project and lessons learned, we adapted and changed the calculations until it was perfect. This is something we continue to do today and it is a phenomenal system that has allowed us to endure and remain in it for the long haul.

As technology changes, the skillset and time required to design and install more complex systems changes as well. We dedicated ourselves to ongoing technical training and within a year we were successfully installing notable projects including Treasure Island Casino right on the Las Vegas strip.

SSI was getting recognized as a legitimate threat and our competition decided to attack us verbally throughout the industry attempting to discredit our capabilities.

I had always told my team: "You're not real if nobody is beating on you." I took their bashing as a huge compliment and knew we had to stay the course, always improving by finding and hiring the best people, while simultaneously growing organically.

We battle with a smile on our faces and never share negative gossip about our competition with vendors or customers.

The '08 economic crash also provided us with another competitive advantage. We realized that many of our customers would not be attending the large trade shows in Vegas, so we decided to take the trade shows to them.

Look at what the masses are doing and create your own differentiators by doing the opposite, in your own unique way.

I have always hated large trade shows. If you have never been to one, imagine massive indoor rooms the size of an airport filled with hundreds of booths with thousands of attendees.

At first glance you might think that sounds like the place to be if you want to get noticed, but here is the challenge. You're standing in your booth that cost you thousands of dollars to buy, you set it up in your little ten foot space that cost you thousands of dollars to rent, paying employees thousands of dollars to travel, giving out thousands of dollars of t-shirts or some other freebie, and the one person you really want to talk to walks by your booth in a sea of bodies and you miss the opportunity to connect.

We decided to create our own tech shows and hosted an event in all nine of our sales regions. We invited key manufacturer partners to participate who could share the costs and reap the benefits of a targeted market segment.

All our tech shows were held in the conference areas of various casinos. We hosted a fantastic lunch with refreshments. Our guests could come and gain essential information, eat a great meal, network with other industry experts, and share time with their SSI family. Nobody had to travel to Vegas which kept expenses low, while the benefits of the event were high.

These shows provided us with unique events to promote and created time for us to build stronger customer relationships. More importantly, we were the first to do it, so if anyone else tried, they would just look like posers. It was another way for us to build up endurance in the marketplace.

With the best possible customer experience in mind, every year we try to improve the experience and create lasting memories with our customers.

Last year we held many of our tech shows at iconic baseball parks around the US and Canada. Wrigley Field was one of my favorites. It was so cool to have our show, then walk into this historical ballpark with our customers to watch a game.

We have had our tech shows at Top Golf, we cruised Lake Michigan on a massive yacht and fished the Gulf Coast. People don't care what you say but they always remember how you make them feel. We created memories with our customer that will last lifetimes.

Another unique experience we created came from my obvious disdain for trade shows. There is a security conference that is held in Vegas every year. It is very surveillance-centric and many of our customers attend it.

We would attend this expensive show, spending our valuable time and money, just to sit in an empty room looking at each other while the customers we want to talk to are locked up in a conference for three days. The only time we would get to see them was when there was a lunch break or during the few hours set aside for exhibitors.

The conference host established a very strict set of guidelines for exhibitors that restricted us from the type of interactions we wanted. So, we did what we do best, disrupt the norm and do something different.

Every year, on the second evening of the conference, we host a massive party reserving the entire top floor of a popular bar/restaurant that overlooks the Vegas strip. We invite all our customers to come join us for an open environment with an assortment of foods, refreshments, and great association.

We also bring in a world-famous UFC fighter to take pictures with every attendee, sign autographs and join us for fun. We have had multiple halls of fame fighters and the party has become the hit of the conference.

Of course, this infuriated the conference host who wanted to control every minute of the attendee's time, even though our party did not conflict with anything he had scheduled. This party has become our main event of the year and is talked about all year long by our customers.

Recently the host decided to restrict SSI and all other integrators from exhibiting, with the exception of one special competitor.

We responded with a smile on our face and searched for ways to still bring unique value to our customers. Our team scheduled tours and demonstrations at premier casinos on the strip that just happen to now be SSI customers.

We have grown from a single casino on the strip to dominating the entire strip just in the last five years. How you ask? I'll get to that part of the story later.

These tours infuriated the conference host who took to publicly bashing SSI and specifically me. How did I respond? I remained positive and smiled with confidence knowing SSI is right on track! You're not real if nobody is bashing you!

Looking back, 2008 was one of the most important years in our eighteen-year history even though revenue dropped by seven million dollars. It forced me to take full control of my company. We dialed in our vision and committed to the process. We were in it for the long haul.

My team stepped up and did exactly what the doubters said we could never do. We came together closer than ever before and became an unstoppable force.

I decided we needed laser focus and that we were not going to try to be all things to all people. We would pursue total domination of the gaming industry while providing the best possible customer experience.

We would always do the best for our customers and never sacrifice our values for short term gain. We would grow and create opportunity for the team that got us to where we are today while looking to strengthen our SSI family with new winners who would share our same vision and values. If we failed, we would fail doing what was right, but we all knew that failure was never an option.

I love Napoleon Hill's books and he has some of my favorite quotes. "Every adversity, every failure, every heartache carries with it the seed of an equal or greater benefit." It is fascinating to see how people react to adversities. Is the glass half empty or is the glass half full?

Realists say that optimists just see life through rose colored glasses. Optimists say that realists are just negative doomsayers who always think the world is falling apart. There is a yin for every yang.

Some of the greatest ideas come from opposing thinkers. If all you do is surround yourself with "yes men" you will rob yourself of the best ideas and strategies and end up mediocre.

Hash out ideas and put them through the ringer until you discover the best, most thought out plan. If everyone doesn't agree, you must still disagree but commit to the new strategy.

Take counsel from people who think differently than you do so you stand a better chance of seeing adversities from all angles, then you can look for and find the seed of equal or greater benefit that you're looking for, without putting you, your family and your company in dangerous situations.

One of the best lessons I have learned is an acceptance of understanding what I know and what I don't know. I do not try to pretend. I either add people to my team that are experts in areas I am not, or I seek counsel from people who have the experience in areas that I don't.

Necessity is the mother of invention. The ancient Greek philosopher Plato said, "A need or problem encourages creative efforts to meet the need or solve the problem."

Anybody can become a solution-oriented person, and you can teach others to do the same. As the leader in your household or your business, people will always come to you looking for answers.

It's beautiful what can happen when you instruct that person to take the emotion out of the situation, take some time to come up with a couple possible solutions, then come back with the solutions so you can talk them through them.

Not only are you teaching people to think differently, but some amazing ideas can be crafted through creative thinking. You will not be required to have all the answers when your team participates in the process.

Another great benefit is that the process promotes emotional stability by shifting your mind from a position of stressful limited thinking, to a calmer, more creative thinking mentality.

In fact, you might even live longer. Long term stress can cause heart attacks, strokes, and other unhealthy conditions. Share the load with your team and you will have time to do other, more creative things. The great news is how we think and how we react is something we have full control over and when we rid ourselves of unnecessary stress and burdens our companies do not just endure, we do as well.

CHAPTER 19

RULERS, LEADERS AND FOLLOWERS

HOW MANY OF US ARE LIVING UP TO OUR TRUE POTEN-tial in anything we do? Science has taught us that the average person is only using 10% of his or her brain's potential.

Regardless if this is just a myth, or not, I believe most people through any self-reflection would agree that they have far more in the tank than what they are using.

I have heard or read various statistics throughout my life regarding the 95% versus 5% as it pertains to human performance, wealth, and influence.

During my short career in the insurance business I was taught that 95% of Americans will be either dead, broke, or still working at the age of 65, while only 5% will be financially independent, not relying on family or the government to live.

In Robert Kiyosaki's book *Cashflow Quadrant* he uses a great illustration to describe this topic. Picture a cube divided into four equal squares. The upper left quadrant is titled "employee." The lower left quadrant is titled "self-employed." The upper right quadrant is titled "business owner." The lower right quadrant is titled "investor."

The left side of the quadrants, the employee and the self-employed, must be actively involved in exchanging time, energy, and effort in order to earn an income. While the right side, the B-quadrant business owner and the investor have the ability to create passive income.

Kiyosaki states the 95% of the population work on the left side sharing only 5% of the wealth, while on the right side is only 5% of the population who share 95% of the wealth.

I believe most people would prefer to earn passive income. That is money which no longer requires their time, energy, and effort to earn.

Passive income is the result of compounding time or money that works for us 24 hours a day. How is it then that 95% of the population ends up employed by the 5% who are business owners?

A quick Google search turned up some information in Wikipedia that describes the "herd mentality."

Researchers at Leeds University performed a group experiment where volunteers were told to randomly walk around a large hall without talking to each other. A select few were then given more detailed instructions on where to walk.

The scientists discovered that people end up blindly following one or two instructed people who appear to know where they are going.

The results of this experiments showed that it only takes 5% of confident looking and instructed people to influence the direction of the 95% of people in the crowd. The 200 volunteers did this without even realizing it.

Does this same herd mentality hold true when it comes to performance and lifestyle as well? I believe it does.

Human nature will mislead us into taking the path of least resistance seeking pleasure instead of pain, so we typically just follow in the footsteps of our parents. If they had a job, you get a job. If they owned a business, you start a business. There is absolutely nothing wrong with having a job, working for somebody else.

If it is true that 95% of the population is selling their time for money working for the 5%, then how can you become a high performer and top earner in the 95% group? I am not suggesting that you can't have a fantastic life working for someone else. Not everybody should be an entrepreneur.

Become the best intrapreneur you can be! I know many people who have become millionaires while working as an employee. You can build a fantastic life for yourself as an employee if you are willing to adopt an owner's mindset.

When you walk into a gym, it doesn't take long to see who the top performers are. Evaluate any company and it is easy to identify who the top performers are.

The same holds true for any sports team I have ever been a part of or any organization I've ever belonged to. There are just certain people who have figured out how to be the best at what they do.

The first step to becoming a top performer and living the life you want is to stop comparing. There is no true joy in comparison. There will always be someone who has it better and someone who has it worse than you. Mediocrity loves to compare, don't let it.

If you waste your time looking at social media, you will be bombarded by people who are attempting to create the illusion of their best life. They take pictures of the food they are eating, videos of the vacations they are on, selfies with ten filters that make them look prettier, skinnier, and sexier.

Then at the same time you see people posting pictures of others who are incredibly poor, or they will even post memes making fun of degenerates. You can see extremes in both cases.

The voyeurs who are looking at this garbage end up comparing themselves to this nonsense and conclude that they do not have it so bad after all.

They have a good job and live in a good house. They are not the skinniest, but they are not as fat as others. They may not be the most beautiful, but they are prettier than others. They are not the richest, but they have it better than someone else. You know the routine. It is a dangerous cycle.

This mentality results in someone becoming a "settle for" person. You put your dreams and ambitions away. Why even try if success will never happen for you?

The "settle for" people start looking for easy solutions like the magic weight loss pill or the get rich quick program. They end up settling for good when they possess what it takes to be great. Simply put, they wallow in and settle for mediocrity instead of trying to master it.

The real question is are you willing to pay the same price as the 5%? All it takes is to change how you think and then fight like crazy to create forward progress every day employing the compound effect.

The same principles apply to business. When the 2008 recession hit, we had built a good business. Lisa and I were making a little bit of money and our lifestyle was far better than it was when we were destitute.

I was proud of what we had achieved and maybe getting a little too comfortable. Getting comfortable can be a dangerous place, and I was at risk of settling for and staying where we were.

Sometimes it takes a good punch in the gut to gain perspective. I feel like I am at my best when facing adversity or I have an enemy to fight. I become more creative and definitely more driven.

I'm not sure if my drive comes from a fear of failure or my desire to prove people wrong.

When it comes to motivation and goals, we are all either running from something or running towards something, or a combination of both.

In my case, it has depended on where I was in life at that specific time. During the 08' crisis, there was no chance I was going to let my business slide backwards and fail. There was no way I was going to let down the people I love.

I turned to my SSI family. I rallied our team together and reinforced our purpose with clear direction. We went back to the basics of making a hundred calls each and every day. We stepped up our customer interactions and looked for creative ways to improve customer experience. We cut costs so we could save money to hire unique talent, if and when, they became available.

SSI was well established on the West Coast, so we upped our efforts in the East. The increase in our activity combined with a more narrowed focus reaped us much improved results.

Because of our intense focus and effort, we steadily gained ground on our competition. We took advantage of every mistake they made. We were winning one customer at a time. We remained hyper focused for two years, and when preparedness intersected with opportunity, we caught a lucky break.

Years ago, I read the parable of the king and the poisoned well. In a city far away there lived a king who ruled his people with strength and understanding. In the middle of the city was a fresh water well where everybody would drink, including the king.

One day an outsider came to town and poisoned the well. Everybody who drank from the well went crazy with madness.

The king was told about the poisoned water, but he did nothing about it. By the next day most of the city had already gone mad.

People began talking about the king's odd behavior. The mad township started a rebellion and decided to overthrow and kill the king.

Right before he was to be attacked, the king drank from the well so he could be seen as normal and be accepted by his people. Rather than continuing to lead with strength, he decided to just blend in with his people.

I am going to twist this parable a little to re-tell a story I have witnessed many times over with different casts and characters. The story goes something like this...

In a city far away, there was a business where the founders had built a thriving company. The culture they nurtured was based on graceful strength, understanding and teamwork.

The founders had built something very special, but they were ready to make a change in their lives. Soon after, the company sold.

The new owner moved into the city and appointed himself as the new king. The new king was very ego driven and decided to change the culture to serve his own needs. People resisted change so the king decided to slowly poison the well from where everyone drank.

Not enough poison to kill them, just enough to make them sick. Then insidiously, the king incentivized with a cure. If you do as I say and loyally follow me, I can take away your sickness and you will feel good.

What leader in their right mind would poison their own well? Seems crazy, but we see it all the time. It could be a parent who puts their own needs ahead of the family. It could also be a CEO who feels that the employees are only there to serve his needs and they should just be grateful to have a job.

It might be a dictator who terrorizes his people and is willing to torture and kill them to gain control. In my lifetime, I have witnessed many fantastic companies sell.

Then, the new owners come in and destroy the culture driving the company to failure. Winners never want to be ruled and will choose to leave the oppression behind.

There are people who are life enhancers and those who are well poisoners. The king in the first story chose to fit in with the masses by drinking the poisoned water rather than stand alone and fight to change how people think.

The king in the second story chose to force people to think the same as him so he could rule them. Well poisoners never create lasting success or healthy cultures. Rulers are not leaders.

Talent acquisition can be one of the most challenging tasks when growing a thriving business. Often times, talented employees leave companies that have sold because they just don't fit in to the new culture.

Others use the timing as an opportunity to make personal improvements and seek change. Sometimes we just get lucky and come across some of these very talented people who are looking for a change and greater opportunity.

We will only attract these people if we have already nurtured a winning culture, not a mediocre one filled with poisoned wells, rulers, and herd mentalities.

I had heard rumors that a very talented salesperson may be looking for new opportunities. This guy had been kicking my butt in Vegas for years. We would be blessed to have him join the SSI family.

I had no idea how to get in touch with him. I turned to LinkedIn so I could direct message him. I pulled up the profile for Daniel Jackson, the Aussie stud who had Vegas on lockdown.

Over his lifetime DJ had developed incredibly strong relationships and loyalty from his customers. I knew he was a positive team player and would be a perfect cultural fit for SSI.

I decided to throw a hail Mary pass and send him a quick direct message. I told DJ that I had heard he was taking some time off to weigh out his future options. I let him know how much I respected what he had accomplished, and if he decided to work for another integrator, I would love to talk to him.

He kindly responded confirming that he was going to take a year off so he could decide what he was going to do with his life. I thanked him and wished him well.

In the meantime, SSI continued to grow. We had become a highly recognized company in the security industry winning national awards for revenue growth. We had been blessed to be published in many magazines for the work we were doing in the gaming industry.

The part that I am most proud of, is our reputation with customers and suppliers. SSI is recognized as a company that treats our employees like family. We work well together as a team, always looking out for one another.

We make it a priority to provide the best possible employee experience and do our best to make winning fun! I am extremely proud of my team and I see them as my work family, as dysfunctional as we are.

I love what I do and enjoy every day at work. It is incredibly rewarding to win with the people you care about. Ours is no mediocre culture.

A year had quickly passed and for some reason DJ's name popped up in my head. I decided to reach out to him once again.

He quickly responded that he had decided to get back into the industry and he was open to talking. We exchanged phone information and set an appointment to speak. We had a great conversation. DJ is a very positive, energetic person who places a high importance on family values.

He shared with me that he loved the idea of once again working within a family-based business. He had checked out our reputation and had only heard great things.

I invited DJ to fly to Sacramento so he could visit our HQ in Rocklin and meet our people. The following week DJ came into town and he felt right at home. We had a great visit. He and Melissa hit it off. We cut a deal and that day and DJ joined our family.

DJ had been in the security industry his whole life working for a few other integrators before he had landed at our biggest competitor.

DJ was responsible for selling the majority of the Las Vegas strip and he had beat us out on projects time and time again. To have this guy now on our side was a game changer.

It seemed the entire Vegas strip was pregnant with the Honeywell systems DJ had sold in previous years. Up until this time we had sold very little Honeywell because DJ had been dominating us and Honeywell protected the business DJ had developed. I was not sure how we could support systems we had never sold, but we were willing to do whatever it took to support his customers.

SSI had been and always will be a sales company first. I believe everything we need to know to succeed lives in our customers heads. So, we listen to the market and respond accordingly, always maintaining a nimble and agile stance.

The market was saying that I had better learn how to support Honeywell if we wanted any chance to compete for the business of the Vegas gaming giants.

DJ called me to let me know that Honeywell was realigning some divisions and a gentleman who had provided him support for decades had somehow become available.

DJ made the introduction to Greg Stowers, a Texas native who has been in the security industry for close to three decades. I doubt there is anyone in the U.S. who understands Honeywell systems better than Greg. It was clear that Greg would be a gamechanger for SSI in our pursuit of large, technical casino projects.

Once again, we were blessed to hire another highly talented person. Greg's analytical nature combined with empirical knowledge has guided us safely through some of the biggest casino projects in America.

By adding these new thoroughbreds to our existing stable of industry stars, we were quickly becoming a dominant force.

By 2014 we had fought our way to the top and SSI was recognized by Security Business Magazine as #18 in the 50 fastest growing security companies in America. With our continued growth and the addition of new team members in 2018, SBM recognized SSI as #2 in the 50 fastest growing security companies in America.

It was a mere dream for many years just to make any list and obtain any recognition. To be recognized by SBM on this list was a dream come true. We are a proud, but humble company. I am blessed to have the team we have, and I will always fight the good fight with these people.

I will always do what is right for the team first before I do anything that benefits me personally. This practice keeps our motives pure and we avoid the mistake of putting profits ahead of people.

Ultimately, it allows me to be a leader, not a ruler and the citizens of our kingdom are all the better for it!

CHAPTER 20

BUILDING A FAMILY BUSINESS

MANY PEOPLE SEEM AMAZED WHEN THEY FIND OUT that I have family working in the business, especially my kids. It has been the practice of many CEOs to prevent their children from working in their businesses in order to avoid the perception of nepotism. Nepotism in any business results in an us and them environment creating division within the team.

I have heard stories of failure when kids work in the family business if they are allowed to operate outside the lines. I love the movie Tommy Boy. After six years in college Tommy, played by the hilarious Chris Farley, barely graduates with a D+, something I can relate to, and comes home to work in the family car parts business.

Tommy is picked up at the airport by Richard, played by David Spade. Richard clearly has a chip on his shoulder since he has been grinding it out for years working for Tommy's father who now rewards Richard by placing him in charge of babysitting Tommy Boy.

Tommy has no practical experience and he has a reputation as a screw up, but he is handed his own office and minifridge. Richard is instructed to look out for Tommy and show him the ropes.

This satirical comedy is full of insulting banter and has a happy ending, however this type of nepotism happens every day.

It is common occurrence for a business to be handed off to the founder's children just to see it driven into the ground. CEOs who either pressure their kids to join the family business or who just allow them to join without paying a price both make the same mistake, and both result in failure.

In my opinion, you cannot raise children one way and then expect them to act different in the workplace. The same dynamic will exist.

I believe the only way to create a healthy dynamic in a family business is to set the precedent when they are children for them to not succumb to mediocrity. This involves setting the expectation that they will not get a pass

For us it started when I began coaching our kids in sports. Melissa was a pitcher in girl's fastpitch softball while Michael, Austin and Masen primarily played football.

I made it perfectly clear that they would have to outperform the other players in order to earn playing time and a starting position. I engrained in their minds that a tie goes to the other player. I never wavered on this rule and it was up to them to fight for what they wanted.

I was never going to be one of those parents or coaches who played my kids over more talented players. I have personally experienced this as a youngster and as an adult. It is unfair to all involved.

The athlete who has outworked and is more talented feels slighted and may be permanently damaged by the coach who screws him over.

It is equally unfair to the coach's child who now learns that daddy will help him when he doesn't deserve it. This decision will rob the child of the recognition when he does well because deep down, he knows he didn't earn it and typically the coach glorifies the kid with too much recognition in attempt to justify his own poor decision. The coach then applies massive pressure on the kid to perform beyond his abilities to perpetuate the lie.

Isn't it crazy for a CEO to do the same thing in business, put the young adult in a position he doesn't deserve then apply massive pressure? It is insanity to do the same things over and over expecting different results. Everybody sees the madness, except for the coach (CEO) and the kid (young adult).

The rule Lisa and I had for all our children while attending high school was that they would either play a sport or get a job. There will be no sitting at home playing video games or just goofing around doing nothing.

When Melissa made the decision to stop playing softball to focus on her grades, she was required to get a job. She started out scooping ice cream in a crummy neighborhood for a short time before getting a job in a local deli. She worked there for a couple years before coming to work for me.

That was the second rule. If you want to work in the family business, you would be required to work somewhere else for two years to get a sense of the real world.

Melissa, while in high school, also worked for me at Northern Video starting in the warehouse and eventually earning her way as my assistant. Shortly after starting SSI Melissa left the deli business and joined the family business in a sales assistant role.

Melissa worked full time while earning her bachelors, and while she fast-tracked her masters. Melissa is an incredibly driven, smart, and motivated person who continues to impress and challenge me every day.

It was a natural transition for her to advance in sales and it was not long before she was a top sales producer. Not only did she lead SSI in sales, she worked with me on developing systems and structure for the entire sales department.

Melissa knows every aspect in the business and has performed many roles over the years. She has grown into one of my few trusted advisors, and I respect her decision making.

As the company continued to grow, she was the perfect choice to replace the VP that I had to let go. The company had simply outgrown his abilities and he was unwilling to change.

Melissa took over the role with ease and to this day she is highly respected by her peers. Melissa is married to AJ and together they are raising three amazing girls, Alexandra, Reagan, and Savannah.

Michael is my oldest son and has had to follow in the footsteps of a high achiever. This is not an easy task for anyone, but Michael was determined to make his own way in life.

He too wanted to join the business, but he too had to serve his time in the outside world. Michael worked for a local gym for two years before he was hired at SSI as an entry level installer.

He joined SSI in the early days when we were still trying to figure out who we wanted to be. He had no technical background; he was going to have to learn in the trenches.

When Michael first started, he was a wire puller, but to advance he would need to learn how to install a complete security system. SSI was selling anything we could at the time, so he had to learn to perform in multiple environments with a broad spectrum of equipment.

In his early days Michael was the guy who had to crawl up in the filthy ceilings to pull cable. Michael is 6'1' and 250 lbs. That's a big body to squeeze through tight crawl spaces!

He was getting dirty and paying his dues. Meanwhile SSI continued to grow, and Michael's abilities continued to improve. He had become a very sound installer and was able to manage projects on his own.

During this time SSI was quickly moving east, and I wanted to establish a presence in Oklahoma. There are approximately 102 casinos in Oklahoma alone, so if we were going to dominate gaming, we were going to need a physical presence.

To my dismay, Michael volunteered to open our new branch in Tulsa. Although I did not want my son to move away, I was very proud that he was willing to make the sacrifice to support the business. Michael stayed in Oklahoma for two years to establish the new location, but he was clamoring to come home.

Michael had completed some very large casino projects and had become technically astute. When he got home, Michael informed me that he wanted to transition from field services to sales.

We had an opening in the Pacific Northwest, but I was highly concerned that this would be too big of a jump for Michael.

People who do not know him would consider Michael to be quiet and shy. These are two words not normally associated with a salesperson, but Michael was motivated to get married and start a family.

He believed he could make more money in sales. I would never hold anyone back from self-improvement, so I gave him the chance to sell. He would have to travel for a week or two at a time in order to service the PNW. Soon enough, he started to gain traction that resulted in new sales.

Michael's experience as an installer along with his quiet demeanor created the perception that he was more an advisor than a salesperson. Michael decided to move to Washington to better establish our presence in the state. He stayed for two years and did a very solid job.

Michael has developed into a skilled salesperson and is responsible for landing one of the largest accounts in the country. Michael achieved his dream and married a beautiful woman. Today, Michael and Lauren are raising two fine boys, Declan, and Grayson.

Austin, my middle son, is such an amazing character. He has always danced to the beat of his own music and is incredibly funny. While in high school Austin also wanted to join the business, but I felt he was too young.

He was very persistent, so I altered my rules of entry just a little. I did not require Austin to work in the outside world, I had a better plan for him.

I gave him a dirty job in the warehouse that would surely motivate him to get a job somewhere else. We had a very large warehouse located in an old building that we had recently moved into.

I instructed Austin to clean every inch of the warehouse space and take inventory of all the old used and outdated inventory. Austin jumped all over the job without complaint.

He was out there for about a week before he approached me with an idea to sell all the outdated product on eBay, and he tried to negotiate a small commission for his efforts.

I agreed, believing he would not sell any of that junk. To my pleasant surprise he was making sales daily, and in a short time, he had sold it all. Now he had a taste for selling and he was convinced that he was a natural.

While still in high school, he wanted to work part time in the big boy sales department. Since I do not employ any part time salespeople, I offered him a position making cold calls for a salesperson who was struggling to book anything on his own. Austin agreed and on the very first day he booked three new appointments for the guy.

I was surprised and assumed it was just an anomaly. However, he continued to book new appointments day after day and was never shaken by the grind of cold calling. I thought that maybe this kid was a natural salesperson.

Austin graduated high school and started college while continuing to bang the phones making marketing calls. Austin had so much success that Melissa and I agreed that he had earned a chance to work his own CRM, in an associate sales position.

Ensuring that he was going to pay his own price of entry, his sister made sure Austin was provided with a list of prospects that were dead in the water.

Austin responded like a champ, selling accounts we never thought he could sell. He was building his own customer base, so we did what we do with every salesperson. When you prove yourself through consistent action and attitude, you get rewarded with healthier leads.

Austin continued building momentum all through college until he graduated earning his Bachelors of Art in Business Administration. Austin was responsible for putting SSI on the map out on the East Coast.

He has continued to grow into one of the most successful sales leaders in the industry. A few years ago, Austin was promoted to East Coast Director of Sales. He married his high school sweetheart Morgan and they are raising their son, Dax.

Now we come to the baby of the family, Masen. We all know the youngest sibling never has to pay the same price as the oldest. What can I say, times change and my parenting skills diminished, according to his siblings.

There is no question that Melissa had to pay the toughest price being raised by twenty-two-year-old parents who had no clue what they were doing while living through financial self-destruction. Masen does not have a single memory of our poverty and will be the first one to say he doesn't care.

Masen has the task of following in the footsteps of three successful siblings, but as a millennial he walks outside the lines. Masen is a very smart, strong-willed young man who has the potential to do whatever he decides to commit himself to.

Masen, like the others, decided he wanted to work at SSI with the rest of the family. I was very unsure that this would be a good idea. Everything was working fine, and I was concerned that adding a fourth kid to the mix could ruin the recipe.

During his senior year in high school, after football was over, Masen just like the others, was required to get a job. He went to work for the same gym that Michael worked at, doing the exact same job. After two years Masen grew tired of cleaning gym equipment and was begging me for a chance to prove himself.

I knew he had the brains, but I wasn't sure he had the commitment. I reluctantly agreed, but I knew I was going to need to make him pay a big price to gain the acceptance of his siblings.

I told Masen that he could come to work, but he was going to have to work for free for six months before I would add him to the payroll. I was already paying for his gas and his college education, plus he was still living at home so I knew mommy would not let him starve. Shockingly he agreed to the terms!

The first day on the job Masen came in early and jumped all over the phones. I was pleasantly surprised. I questioned if his commitment would last. It has. He still comes in early and has a very teachable spirit. He has been a quick learner and has brought value to the team. We have a blast and he makes us laugh every day.

He has started building a nice customer base too and he has a great future ahead of him. I can't wait to see where his journey takes him. Masen has incredible potential.

I share these stories about my children only to illustrate the point that none of them walked through the front door and were handed an office and a mini fridge. That is an approach that only fosters complacency of course our good friend mediocrity.

Each has had to pay their own, unique price and prove themselves to be worthy of the respect of their peers. They know that a tie goes to the other player and they will never be handed a starting position over someone else who deserves it more.

We have a rule that all family matters remain at the front door of SSI and all business matters remain at the door of our homes. We work very hard to never mix the two unless we are celebrating victories.

Do we have a perfect situation all the time? Absolutely not. We have made many mistakes, but we always lean into the principles that have made our family dynamic work. I am a truly blessed man because I get to build the business of my dreams with the people I love most.

I have already spoken of a few people who have been part of our SSI family and a few who had joined the team as we progressed.

The last thing I want to do is overlook those team members who have been incredibly loyal and important to our cause.

You know who you are. We only win if everybody plays their position with all they have. I appreciate you and will always be grateful. We have and will continue to master mediocrity together!

CHAPTER 21

CRISIS MANAGEMENT

2018 AND 2019 WERE BOTH RECORD YEARS. THE PRE-vious 18 years of grinding matured at the exact same time we were winning the most prestigious casino projects in America.

SSI was winning the war of attrition against its competitors. To this day we have stayed true to the SSI mission without violating key principles, both human and financial.

We have been blessed to become the new home for some incredibly talented people as some of our earliest competitors have failed.

Our field services team has evolved through the analog to digital age without our customers feeling the pain of the learning curve. I'm so proud of the quality of work we are producing today.

Our inside sales team that was once seen from outsiders as nothing more than a telemarketing group has evolved into a force to be reckoned with.

Little did the doubters know that our sales team has been dedicated to learning for over a decade, grinding out their 10,000 hours to mastery. They now possess the ability to produce system designs better than our previous, haughty engineering team did back in 2008.

It is extremely challenging to generate long lasting momentum, but after 18 years of compounded effort we have perpetuated SSI to be a dominant, international casino integration company as we have trampled over mediocrity in the quest for success.

When SSI transitioned from 2019 to 2020, it seemed like it was going to be another record year. When looking at our SWOT (strengths, weaknesses, opportunities, and threats) analysis, who knew that a major threat would come from an unknown enemy.

Many companies start over every January 1st with zero sales. The momentum we had created allowed SSI to travel from year to year without broken focus caused by major dips in sales. Sometimes we were doing everything right and then something we never planned for hit us with a sucker punch.

When news of the Coronavirus (COVID-19) started to find its way into our homes and businesses, the world seemed to freeze with fear. In the beginning, it seemed like this was just something infecting China, but it did not take long to realize it would attack the U.S. as well.

Scientists and epidemiologists had been predicting a pandemic for years, however it appeared that most of the world, including America, wasn't prepared for it.

When there is so much uncertainty and fear, the medical community is forced to respond in the only way they know how. We fall back to the practice of full quarantines.

The practice of quarantine, as we know it, began during the 14th century in an effort to protect coastal cities from plague epidemics.

Ships arriving in Venice from infected ports were required to sit at anchor for 40 days before landing. In 1738 New York commandeered Bedloe's Island, the current home of the Statue of Liberty, and turned it into a quarantine station to prevent the spread of smallpox and yellow fever.

Ships arriving from foreign countries were also transporting disease carrying rats or people who were unknowingly infected which required sever precautionary measures.

In today's fast paced world people are not traveling from one country to another by ship, they are traveling the world by airplane. A virus can spread from patient zero to other countries within days creating a worldwide pandemic.

I would have never dreamed that Americans would be ordered to shelter in place. It is bizarre to leave the house wearing a mask just to go to the market to purchase essentials.

The stock market crashed, millions of people have been laid off from work, unemployment is skyrocketing, and people are relying on the Federal government for bailout money.

As a leader, how you respond during a crisis will define you. Will you turn obstacles into opportunity and fight another round, or will you stay seated when the bell sounds? Will you succumb to mediocrity's temptation to settle?

Leadership development is a multi-billion-dollar industry. There are more resources available today than ever in history pertaining to leadership through books, seminars, podcasts, associations, videos, and professional coaching.

I have invested thousands of hours ingesting everything I can to grow as a person and as a leader. I am not even going to attempt to act like I'm an expert on the topic, but I do have some real-life experiences to lean on.

I am going to speak specifically about leadership during a crisis. Leaders are forged in crisis. Most American people have never been truly tested in life and have no idea how to respond when the world seems to be falling apart around them.

There are some exceptions, like combat veterans and first responders. These unique individuals have had a tremendous amount of training and experience while under, what to most of us seems like insurmountable pressure.

There are also some people who just seem to be wired to handle it better than others. Is it possible that it is the same group of people who had very difficult childhoods and learned how to survive? Did the pain and struggle forge them into natural leaders who can handle extreme stress and pressure? I can't speak for the world, but I believe that is the case for me.

I am not suggesting that every person who had a tough childhood comes out the other side as a leader. Some come out the other side as psychopaths and criminals. I was just lucky enough to have a solid support system around me that acted like bumper rails in a bowling alley.

My job was to keep the ball rolling, their job was to keep me in the lane. My wife Lisa has always been one of those people for me and I thank God every day for her.

As I am writing this chapter the entire world is under attack from an invisible killer. The virus has no prejudices, people of all ages can be infected, but it prefers to attack people with weak immune systems.

Older people, and people with pre-existing medical conditions (such as asthma, diabetes, and heart disease) appear to be more vulnerable. It has quickly become a worldwide pandemic with its origins in China. It spread through Asia and Europe and within weeks made its way to America.

There has been a massive amount of sensationalism by the media that has fed the fear of the unknown and people have reacted with hysteria and panic. Consumers converged on grocery stores hoarding essentials like water, toilet paper and hand sanitizer.

Old ladies were fist fighting on the grocery aisle over the last roll of paper towels. Criminals attacked people in the parking lot robbing them of their groceries. I could not believe what I was watching happen.

Most conversations have been negative, only contributing to greater fears and fueling more hysteria. The insane thing is COVID19 does not affect drinking water or cause diarrhea, so why the craziness with toilet paper? Have we become a country who cannot drink water from a faucet, or figure out an alternative to toilet paper?

In some countries this is daily life, pandemic or not. In many countries you are not allowed to freely move about, and grocery store shelves are always empty, but here in the U.S. you ask people to sequester themselves and stay safe and they lose their minds.

In no way am I downplaying the critical nature of the situation, but it is fascinating to watch the initial reaction of the masses. This is not a fine representation of human nature, and it speaks volumes to the necessity for quality leadership.

Amongst all the negative, we have also witnessed beautiful acts of support and kindness. Families are coming closer together as we take stock of our blessings and what is really important in our lives.

Parents are investing precious time home schooling their children allowing them time to bond in ways they could not before.

Families are eating dinner together again. People are calling their elderly parents and grandparents just to say I love you. Communities are coming together to provide support, food, and medicine to those in need.

In our short history as a nation, Americans will continue to do what we always do when threatened. We come together as a single cohesive unit and work together to fight a common enemy, regardless if it is a foreign enemy or a virus.

We will emerge from this battle stronger than ever before and get back to winning! There will be some very positive changes that come out of this terrible time in history.

Americans have been enjoying the Trump economy, the best we have seen in decades. Unemployment has been at an all-time low and the stock market has been at an all-time high.

On February 12th, 2020, the market closed at 29,551 the highest day on record. Then, the coronavirus hit the U.S. and in less than a month the market plunged. The crash began on March 9, 2020. The Dow fell 2,013 points that day to 23,851, the Dow's worst single-day point drop in U.S. market history.

Companies that had been thriving only weeks earlier were forced to lay off employees. The economy would go on to record high job losses.

It is during the most challenging times that true leadership shines. What will history say about you when this is over? Will you hide yourself away marinating in misery, feeling sorry for yourself, or will you become more visible than ever, serving as the beacon of hope for those who depend on you?

It is easy and fun to lead when riding the wave of momentum and prosperity, but when under attack, the intense pressure requires character and courage.

I love studying history. It is full of stories of leaders who emerged during times of crisis. In September 1940 Hitler unleashed the Luftwaffe in a merciless bombing campaign against London and other major British cities.

Hitler named the air raid campaign the "blitz' which was designed to terrorize the civilians of England. It was Hitler's deadly desire to break the morale of the British people so that they would pressure Churchill into negotiating.

The UK was bombed every day for eight months and over 60% of London was demolished. More than 43,000 civilians were killed and another 139,000 injured during the attacks. You would surmise that this level of death and destruction would achieve Hitler's goal. It had the opposite effect thanks to the leadership of Britain's prime minister Winston Churchill.

Everything we need to know on how to lead during crisis, we can learn from how Churchill responded when London was attacked. He did not hide-away in some underground bunker. Churchill made himself visible to the people every single day.

When he visited a city that had been bombed, the people would flock to him. His visits were essential to helping Britain weather the storm. He was visible on the evening news, written about in the newspapers and listened to on the radio.

Churchill was demonstrating visible leadership. He showed the world that he truly cared, and that he was fearless. Your people need to see you and hear from you, especially when they are getting bombed by the media and are running scared.

Churchill was also incredible at communicating with the people who were looking to him for hope. He was not ambiguous, pumping people full of false hope. He was honest and straightforward without the concern of managing the feelings of his colleagues.

On June 4th, 1940 Churchill delivered his famous speech that history has named *We Shall Fight on the Beaches* to the House of Commons. In a time of great fear and concern his words brought a nation together.

*"Even though large tracts of Europe and many old
and famous States have fallen or may fall into the
grip of the Gestapo and all the odious apparatus of*

Nazi rule, we shall not flag or fail. We shall go on to the end, we shall fight in France, we shall fight on the seas and oceans, we shall fight with growing confidence and growing strength in the air, we shall defend our Island, whatever the cost may be, we shall fight on the beaches, we shall fight on the landing grounds, we shall fight in the fields and in the streets, we shall fight in the hills; we shall never surrender, and even if, which I do not for a moment believe, this Island or a large part of it were subjugated and starving, then our Empire beyond the seas, armed and guarded by the British Fleet, would carry on the struggle, until, in God's good time, the New World, with all its power and might, steps forth to the rescue and the liberation of the old."

Churchills' message was not ambiguous, it was crystal clear. He pulled his country together to fight a common enemy. His call to action changed the course of WWII and world history forever.

During the pandemic I have thought a lot about how CEOs and other leaders are handling the situation, not just the economic crash, but the optics of how they perform while everyone is looking to them for hope.

I wonder if they are providing clear messages and battle cries to their teams. I wonder if their confidence is helping their teams fight forward against the common enemy.

I am sure there are some leaders who are tucked away in their bunkers safe from any danger. Their predominant thoughts are fear-based protectionism, thinking only about how they must protect and keep what they have built for themselves.

Other leaders are probably aching over what to do and how to respond, avoiding communicating until they have the perfect plan. They do not want to appear weak and indecisive, so they don't say anything. Truly mediocre! When a leader goes dark and there is no communication, the team will always assume the worst.

The right thing to do is simply reach out to your entire team and let them know how much you genuinely care about them.

Look for ways to help them through the crisis, many times it's the little acts of kindness that mean the most. Share a consistent message of hope and reassure them that you are all in this together and that means in the good and the bad.

Come up with your own battle cry with a call to action. If you wait for the perfect plan during a crisis, it will be too late. Be decisive even though you may not have all the details. Be flexible and willing to adapt as the crisis unfolds.

Do what is right for the greater good of your family and company. Be the first to take a financial hit before you ask the rest of the team to join you. Never share negative language that will create doubt and insecurity in the minds of your people.

I'm not suggesting you avoid the realities of the situation. I'm suggesting you attack them head on, without the perfect plan, never wavering in your optimism.

People don't care what you know, until they know that you care. Be a servant leader and your team will be there with you when the crisis is over while mediocrity is nowhere in sight.

Leader is a verb not a noun. It is not the title on the business card or the stripes on the uniform that make a leader. A leader is someone who takes action when others are paralyzed with fear.

A key leadership trait during challenging times is emotional stability. It is critical to understand that human nature is never our friend and we have to fight against emotional knee-jerk reactions.

My nature has always been to be a reactionary person, a trait that can be both good and bad. When that emotion is controlled, it assists me in making quick decisions. I trust my instincts. The key to its effectiveness has been developing the habit of removing the emotion from the situation, only addressing the facts.

During a crisis we are surrounded by emotional instability, and understandingly so. People are scared. The fear of the unknown can rattle people to their core. One of my techniques is to address the worst-case scenario first, which is likely not to happen, taking the scenario off the table.

Then I place myself in a mindset of gratitude. I think about what I am grateful for and often times verbally thank God for my own challenges.

I have often said "If it's not chemo, it's not a big deal." People every day are living with life and death situations; those are real challenges. This phrase usually minimizes what I am dealing with and puts things quickly into perspective.

Then, with gratitude in my heart, I focus on possible solutions to the challenge. If I get stuck in the process, I mentally walk away from the challenge and tell my subconscious mind to go to work on a solution. I cannot tell you how many times that the answer has just popped up in my head when I'm not expecting it.

Consistency is another key trait that will create confidence with your team. My team knows when they come to me, how I am going to react to any situation. I never blow my stack, yell, or lose my cool. I do my best to listen intently.

I ask what solutions they have already thought of, and if there aren't any, I ask them to go work on a few. Then, I will request additional time to think it through. This always gives me a chance to take the emotion out of the situation so I can address it with a clear mind.

I strive to be the leader who, in good times and bad, my people can trust to do the absolute best to provide solutions, while keeping their best interests in mind.

This does not mean that I avoid making the hard decisions, but when I must, they know I'm trying to do what is right for the greater good.

Times of crisis can expose the financial literacy of leaders. Building a strong family or a strong business requires a leader to be fiscally responsible. This is a process that must be implemented long before a crisis strikes, otherwise it will be too late.

I heard a statistic recently that brought back a pit in my stomach that I have not felt in years. It stated that the average American family, regardless of age, has very little money left over after paying for the basics, including healthcare, mortgage, and rent payments.

The danger here lies in spending money when the economy is strong instead of increasing savings for emergencies or opportunities.

I have seen this trend repeat itself multiple times in my life, recently in 2008 and now in 2020. I'm no economist, however basic math can do the trick. If you spend all you make, financial ruin is always lurking around the corner.

In 2006-2007 we witnessed people buying bigger homes, their driveways filled with new cars, ski boats and other toys. It was common to witness people taking out a second loan on their home, wasting their equity to finance a lifestyle they had not yet earned. They settled for financial mediocrity.

As soon as the bubble burst in 2008 and over the next two years an excess of five-million people filed for personal bankruptcy. In 2008 alone, 64,318 businesses filed for bankruptcy compared to 28,322 in 2007. People were running their lives and their businesses on fumes taking unnecessary financial risks.

I understand what was going through their minds, I made the same mistakes in the 80s that eventually led to my own financial ruin. When you finance your lifestyle, you will always be enslaved to your lender who will show no mercy when tough times hit.

The average American family carries more than $8,000 in credit card debt. If they would just choose to live a life of delayed gratification, that money could be saved for emergencies. It is critical to build cash reserves but here is the problem.

Back in 2019 Marketwatch reported that a large number of American households are living paycheck-to-paycheck.

Quoting the results of a survey from the American Payroll Association, they reported that 74% of households would find it "somewhat difficult or very difficult if their paychecks were delayed for a week." This is a frightening statistic.

The same financial principles that apply to personal finances apply to business. It is critical to stay lean when you're riding the wave of momentum so you can save money and build a financial war chest.

Fight against the urge to spend money on building a shiny facade around your business in attempt to appear more successful than you really are.

Fight against the urge to pay yourself too much money, especially in those early years. The money that you might spend overpaying yourself could be used to hire that next superstar who could change the whole trajectory of your business.

Managing your brain during a long-lasting crisis is also essential to the overall mental health of your team, both that of your family and business. I know what it feels like to have that constant pit in your stomach that never leaves.

The fear and stress that builds up during a crisis can be debilitating for some people, but for leaders, it is a luxury we cannot afford. In no way am I suggesting that you shouldn't feel "the feels" of the situation.

I'm telling you we had all better learn to manage emotions that will diminish our ability to lead with conviction and that negatively compromises our decision making.

Recognize when you are in a down mood. You never want to make key decisions when you are down. Wait until you are in a better place, then readdress the challenge and look for solutions. You are the author of your own thoughts, and just because you are thinking it, that does not make it a reality.

I am guilty of having thought attacks. This is something I am aware of and have learned to manage. A thought attack happens when you make an assumption or thought about a person or a situation based on your own interpretation. Since we thought it, it must be true.

In a crisis situation it is human nature to make assumptions and think about negatives that haven't even happened. Thought attacks occur when you cannot let it go and it just won't leave your mind.

Stress levels are raised, sleep is lost, relationships get burned and solutions are missed. When this happens, learn to recognize that these are just thoughts, nothing else. Let it go and focus on solutions. The void of negative thoughts creates room for positive thoughts. This is where peace and happiness live.

That pit in your stomach comes with the position you chose as a parent or CEO and it does not need to be shared with everyone.

First of all, most people will never truly understand what you're going through. The only people who will be able to relate, are those other leaders who have already experienced your situation, or other leaders who are experiencing the same thing.

As I mentioned earlier in the book, I'm part of a great organization called EO. Entrepreneurs Organization is a worldwide business organization created to provide support to business leaders.

EO is a global non-profit organization, whose stated mission is to "Engage leading entrepreneurs to learn and grow."

It is broken down into regions, and within those regions are chapters, within the chapters are small groups of 7-10 entrepreneurs called forums. I have been lucky enough to have experienced two different forums since I joined.

During that time, my business has seen some ups and downs, just like many. The main objective in the forum is to share your highs and lows and drill down to the 5% that really matters.

Then other members can "experience share" on how they may have handled a similar situation, without giving direct advice.

The power in this process is that you never feel isolated. You can share what is going on in your life without passing your challenges on to employees or family members who have no ability to help, which would normally only cause them unnecessary worry or stress.

In addition, just identifying important challenges and saying them out loud to other people who are not there to judge in any way, creates a sense of relief and can give you some respite from the problem.

I highly recommend finding yourself a mentor program or organization like EO so you can participate in an association that can help manage your stress as a leader and help you master mediocrity.

One of my friends in EO, Gerald Agustin, owns a business that provides hospice and serves as an overflow for hospitals. He shared a story with us of two elderly men who were both on their death beds at the same time.

The first man spent his life in the auto body repair business and made a decent living. On his final day the room was full of family members, kids and grandchildren who were all crying and broken hearted over the loss of the family patriarch. They were all sharing stories of family memories sometimes laughing at the funny antics grandpa used to do to make them laugh.

The second man was a successful business owner who had built tremendous wealth over his lifetime. He was only joined by three people, his wife and two adult children.

The only conversation taking place was the two adult children arguing over their potential inheritance. There were no memories being shared. No tears, just bitterness.

What a powerful story to help ground us in a time of crisis. No man lies on his death bed looking at his balance sheet or thinking about how much money he has in his accounts.

In the end, the only thing that will really matter are the positive memories of the times we have invested with the people we love most.

As long as we have our family and our health, everything else can be replaced. Don't lose your mind over the challenges that come your way as a leader. Be the person that others can look to for direction, not by what you say, but how you act, especially during a time of crisis. Be a master of mediocrity.

I have learned over time that I can find tremendous emotional stability when facing major issues by refocusing my mind on gratitude.

We can replace things, but we can never replace people. As long as I am not standing over the grave of my wife, kids or grandkids, I am good.

CHAPTER 22

KEEP A CLEAR MIND

I AM A BIG FAN OF EXERCISE. IT HAS ALWAYS BEEN A WAY for me to burn off steam and clear my mind. Not only leaders, but all people should search for something they can do to find some peace from the insanity of daily life.

It is no secret that stress is a killer. Experts say that stress can have very negative impact on your health. Stress increases the risk of heart disease, diabetes, asthma, and high blood pressure. Stress also puts a major strain on your immune system making you much more susceptible to viruses.

The people who are at the highest risk of death are those who have preexisting conditions like those I just described. In addition to all the frightening physical implications, stress also affects our mental state.

Psychological symptoms related to stress include irritability, anger, depression, nervousness, and anxiety. None of these lend themselves to promoting clear thinking as a leader. Stressed out people are like a repellent for positive outcomes and usually detract from solution-oriented thinking.

It is imperative to our physical and mental well-being to find ways to reduce stress not only so we can have a better quality of life, but also so we can lead our families and businesses when times are tough.

My friend and mentor, Wade Simmons, would always remind me that you cannot give away something you do not have, and he shared this example to illustrate his point.

Picture yourself as a bucket of water. People are always coming to you for direction, answers, motivation, love, kindness, understanding, etc. They take their ladles and scoop out what they need, depleting your bucket.

Day after day, they continue to scoop until your bucket is completely empty. You know the person you become when your bucket is empty. I become irritable and negative. I feel tired and fill my mind with thoughts that derail me from my goals.

At low times, I sometimes tend to feel sorry for myself. I have said silly things become like, "You have no idea what I have to go through every day", or my go to "You have no idea the pressure I'm under!"

Can you relate? It is critical that we recognize when our bucket is getting low and find positive ways to refill our own buckets, otherwise we will have nothing to offer to others who really need our help.

Recently I started re-reading a book I enjoyed twelve years ago titled *You can Be happy no Matter What* by Dr. Richard Carlson.

He shares a plan for happiness based on five principles of thought. They include mood, separate realities, feelings, and the present moment. This book has helped me recognize and understand why I'm thinking the thoughts I have and the impact of timing and mood on the content of my thoughts.

I have always battled against thought attacks. I will get something on my mind that I can't let go of. I will think about it constantly until it grows into a powerful, dominant force. This may be the negative side of my ability to exercise extreme focus towards a dream or a goal.

Thought attacks have only occurred when I'm in a down period or negative state of mind. They pull me away from creative, solution-oriented thinking.

The result is that my bucket is becomes completely depleted. All that is left is dusty negative thinking and I'm left walking around angry and ready to tear someone's head off. This is no place for a parent or a CEO. In fact, it is a dangerous state of mind for anyone. Keep your bucket replenished!

I am a huge proponent of what I call forward motion. I am not suggesting that you become an exercise fanatic, but you could commit yourself to doing something every day to get your heart rate up and get a little sweaty.

Create some forward motion in your life and do not let a day go by without some level of activity. I am willing to bet that over time you will start feeling better about yourself and your activity levels will increase.

Take some time and think about some things you can do that have always made you feel better about yourself. Some people love meditation and yoga. I know other people who love working with their hands doing activities like woodworking, sculpting, or painting.

Whatever it is for you, make time for yourself without robbing your family of the time you need to spend with them. If stress reduces your ability to handle normal daily challenges, you will never be equipped to lead during a real crisis.

I have discovered a technique that has been essential for grounding my mental state and that has greatly improved my ability to lead when under duress.

It is something we all have same access to, and it costs nothing. It takes very little time and when shared with others it can spread like a positive virus.

This powerful technique is called gratitude. When I find myself getting a little sideways with worry, I find a quiet place to thank God for the gifts I have been blessed with in my life.

I focus my mind on the people I love and the good things that have happened for us. Mediocrity loves to complain, but gratitude forces it to take a back seat.

I love motivational speaker Ed Mylett. He says that "Life doesn't happen to you, it happens for you." This includes the good things in addition to the bad things.

I also thank God for the challenges I have in my life and I pray for the strength and guidance to lead with peace and joy in my heart. It only takes me a few minutes to pray and to refocus my mind with gratitude.

I always feel better and find myself in a place of confidence knowing that God will never give me more than I can handle. There have been a few times in my life when I have said "God you must really believe in me right now."

I'm not telling you that you have to believe what I believe, I'm telling you what works for me, however you can't convince me that after spending a few minutes in a mental state of gratitude that you don't feel better about yourself and about your future.

In my case, the opposite side of gratitude is worry. When I focus on worry it always results with thought attacks. We know that most of the things we worry about will never happen, but once again human nature is not our friend.

When under duress our fight or flight instinct kicks in and a side effect is worry. What should I do, attack the problem or run from it, or do nothing and just worry about it?

Penn State did a study on worry and here were the results: A whopping 91% of worries were false alarms. And of the remaining

9% of worries that did come true, the outcomes were better than expected about a third of the time.

Five hundred years ago, the French philosopher, Michel de Montaigne said: "My life has been filled with terrible misfortune; most of which never happened."

Shift your mind from worry by empowering gratitude and focus on solutions while your mind is clear, and your heart is full.

All of these techniques, and many more, will serve you well when leading during a crisis, but they will also help you in your daily life.

Many years ago, I read a book by one of my favorite authors called *How to Stop Worrying and Start Living* by Dale Carnegie. Carnegie says that he wrote it because he "was one of the unhappiest lads in New York".

He said that he made himself sick with worry because he hated his position in life. This drove him to find a way to stop worrying.

I want to encourage you to find books, videos or podcasts that will teach you how to make the shift from worry so you can live a meaningful, joy filled life.

CHAPTER 23
PLAY TO WIN

IN PREVIOUS CHAPTERS I SHARED IDEAS REGARDING the critical nature and power of thought. I'm an advocate of developing a positive mental attitude and often recommend books and podcasts that have been of value to me. There is no question that the world would be a better place to live in if there was less negativity going around.

There is one challenge I want to address. There are many positive thinking people who are in a negative financial position that never seem to accomplish much in their lives.

It drives me nuts when I hear broke people say, "don't worry, God will provide." They carefully use faith to mask their laziness and their mediocrity.

God has already blessed most of us with the ability to get up and go to work every day. I believe there is one main differentiator between people who are just surviving versus high achievers. It is their mindset. Low achievers play to not lose, and in turn settle for mediocrity. High achievers play to win.

There are very smart, talented people who fall short of their potential because they are lacking the secret ingredient to success: drive.

They never learn to develop a winner's mindset. Maybe they just are not willing to do the work necessary to develop the talent.

Regardless of the reason, winning or losing is the byproduct of how we think.

Michael Jordan is one of my favorite examples of a person who mastered the winning mindset. For Jordan losing was not an option. He was consumed with winning and was willing to out-work everyone.

He put the Chicago Bulls on his shoulders and transformed them from a mediocre team to a winning dynasty. Jordan became *the* example for other players to elevate their game.

Jordan did not win six NBA championships alone. He demanded excellence from his team. Anything short of 100% effort was not good enough for him. His competitive nature and work ethic were unlike anything his teammates had ever seen. Michael set the example with his actions and made everyone around him better. What about you? Do you inspire other people to be better?

Have you ever heard anyone say "It isn't whether you win or lose, but it's how you play the game that matters" to the winning team? That is something you say to the losers, or to be PC I should say "non-winners."

I agree that winners should win with humility and non-winners should lose with grace and that both should be done with dignity, but I will never agree that we should accept losing as just a part of life.

Losing should never feel good. That is why we call it losing. If losing felt good, we would call it winning. When people teach their kids that losing is OK and winning just is not for everyone, those kids become adults who are ill-equipped for real life.

There are no participation trophies on the battlefield, just coffins. Regardless of age, anyone can develop the mindset of a winner. It starts with your inner dialogue.

There is no human who thinks positive thoughts all the time. That is an unrealistic expectation. However, we can all recognize when we are thinking negatively and simply put a stop to it.

We are in complete control of our thoughts when we are consciously thinking. When you realize you are in a down mood or you're thinking negative thoughts, you do not have to make the leap to positive, just put your mind in neutral for a few minutes.

One technique I use to place my mind in a neutral state is to shift my thinking to a challenge I need to solve or a task I need to accomplish. During that time, I am neither positive nor negative, I am just thinking.

I am now in a state of problem solving or achievement which always feels right for me. It lends itself to positive feelings. Another effective technique that works for me is to do some manual labor, either in a gym or in the outdoors. A good sweat from physical exertion clears my mind and places me in a state of clear thinking and opens the door for winning expectations.

You never hear winners say, "I will try." When people use the phrase "I'll try" they are leaving themselves with an out and are creating a path to failure and mediocrity.

A winner will do whatever it takes for as long as it takes. The word "try" is not a part of their vocabulary, it is a forgone conclusion. You would have never heard Michael Jordan say, "I will try to make the winning shot." He already made that same shot in practice a thousand times. His mind was already prepared to win.

Michael was always looking for a reason to elevate his game against an opponent. He would use something the media said, a comment from an opposing player, or even a smirk from a rival.

He would internalize the situation and make it personal, then he would go to war. What do you internalize that will increase your drive to become the best version of you?

You will never win the race of life with one foot on the gas pedal and one foot on the brake. When a downhill ski racer ejects his body from the starting gate, he only has one thing on his mind, speed. It is man against mountain. An Olympic downhill racer reaches speeds up to 95 mph with no brake pedal. His expectation is to either win or die trying! Are you that committed to winning?

All the positive talk in the world will not help if your actions do not reflect your words. You will not trust your own thoughts. It is essential that you build self-trust.

If you set a goal to lose ten pounds and then eat a big piece of cake, your subconscious mind puts a check in the liar box.

If you force yourself to walk a mile your subconscious puts a check in the trustworthy box. Either way, your subconscious will look for ways to support your actions, so stop lying to yourself.

Establish a pattern of winning by doing what you say you are going to do. Start small with achievable goals, even if it seems silly at the time. For example, set a goal to walk around the block every evening, rain, or shine, this is something anyone can do.

How you feel at the time cannot have any bearing on whether you walk or not. If we only achieve when we feel like it, nobody will win. It is during these times that you build self-trust.

It is bedtime and you remember that you forgot to go on your walk. Your inner dialogue reminds you "You said you were going to do this no matter what."

What you choose to do next will make or break you. If you choose to get out of bed, get dressed, and go on the walk, you have now established a little trust within yourself.

If you make an excuse like "I will walk twice as far tomorrow" and go to bed, you have now reinforced that you can't trust yourself and when you set a goal and you know you won't achieve it. It is critical that you establish a pattern of winning, regardless of the emotion of the moment.

This same technique works in all areas of your life. Broke people make excuses, wealthy people make money. Excuses and winning cannot co-exist in your head.

When you feel an excuse coming on say out loud "I do what I say I'm going to do, before I need to do it, whether I feel like it or not" then immediately take action. Take the walk. Make the sales call. Eat the healthy option. Ask for forgiveness.

Compounded over time, these small victories become natural and you begin to develop the mindset of a winner. Your self-confidence will improve, and you will look for ways to gain an edge.

What used to feel like work will become your new normal. You will embrace struggles because you know that victory lives on the other side.

You already possess the tools to win in life. Learn how to consistently use them and you will achieve your dreams and goals and you will master mediocrity.

CHAPTER 24

BILLY AND SUSIE

THE BIGGER CHALLENGE IS THAT WE LIVE IN A WORLD that encourages mediocrity. As soon as idiots started passing out participation trophies just for showing up, they stopped challenging kids to be great. They robbed the high achievers of the recognition they earned, all so Billy would not get his feelings hurt.

The reality is that the high achiever will likely go on and continue to excel, while Billy who received recognition for being average will continue to struggle.

What a slippery slope for Billy. Now when he is challenged to improve, he will feel attacked and mommy and daddy will have to come to his rescue.

Instead of nurturing Billy's seed of greatness by challenging him to be better, his parents caudle him and try to protect him from the harsh world.

Before you get twisted, I understand that not every kid is an "A" student or all-star baseball player, but every kid can learn to live to his or her full potential and master mediocrity.

Look at Susie, an "A" student who happens to be a chubby, freckle-faced little redhead. She could grow up to become an amazing woman that leads a Fortune 500 company, but Susie spends too much time on social media looking at all the pictures and videos her classmates are posting, not recognizing that they are using fifteen different filters to alter how they really look while pretending to be living their best lives.

All Susie sees are other girls her age that look prettier and skinnier, surrounded by friends, and always having fun. What she does not see are little girls who are growing up way too fast with hopes of getting rich by becoming Instagram models, living lives full of false pretense.

Susie feels like she can never be like those other girls and becomes depressed by her perceived false reality.

So rather than stand out, Susie decides to blend into the crowd because her self-esteem has been damaged by all the fake images and posts that inundated her life. Her grades slip and she is in a constant state of depression because Susie believes that what she sees on the internet represents real life.

Studies have proven that social media is having a greater negative impact on girls than boys and cyberbullying is driving these young babies to not only consider, but actually commit suicide.

Those who do not physically hurt themselves would rather blend in and accept mediocrity as a way of life rather than stand out and run the risk of being bullied.

Behind closed doors, everyone has their own set of issues to overcome. Regardless if they grew up rich or poor, had married or divorced parents, were healthy or sick, somebody made them feel bad for who they are.

Childhood trauma can create scar tissue that can last a lifetime. It is my wish that people can inspire hope for you, regardless of what has happened to you in life. You possess the seed of greatness. You were made in the image of God, and God does not make any junk!

You can choose to be a victim of your circumstances or you can dig deep in your soul for the courage to change and grow to be the best version of you!

We look at famous people and see the result of their grit and struggle. We do not see the struggle. Richard Branson battled dyslexia to become a billionaire. There are Hollywood superstars, professional athletes, and world recognized leaders who have had to overcome learning disabilities, child abuse, alcoholic parents, bullying, all the same challenges you and I have had to deal with.

There have been American President's like Dwight Eisenhower who had a learning disability. Abraham Lincoln lived with depression and James Madison had epilepsy.

There are millions of stories of people who have struggled to overcome the odds to find joy and meaning in life. None of these settled for mediocrity.

Whatever it is in your life that has held you back from achieving your dreams and goals, there is somebody else who has already conquered the same challenge. Look for stories that you can relate to that will help inspire you to take a step forward.

If you choose to fight for your limitations, then you deserve the outcome. Write down this saying and refer to it anytime you are faced with a major challenge. When your dreams and goals hold a greater priority in your life than the obstacles that come your way, you can then overcome any obstacles to reach your dreams and goals.

I once heard a story of a young boy who went with his grandfather to visit his grandmother's grave. As they were walking through the cemetery, like any curious child, the boy asked his grandfather a million questions about his life and the things he had done.

Eventually, they arrived at her site, and as grandpa placed fresh flowers at the headstone of his truest love, his life flashed before his eyes.

He remembered growing up on a small Iowa farm working the fields with his parents. He remembered holding his best friend's hand as he took his last breath on the beach in Normandy. He smiled as he recalled the morning when the boy's mother took her first breath as a beautiful newborn baby. Images flashed through his mind at the speed of light as he remembered all the highs and lows of his long life.

The little boy noticed the smile had left his grandfather's face and was replaced by a single tear that made its way down is wrinkled cheek.

They sat quiet for a moment staring at the headstone until the boy broke the silence with another question. "Grandpa, what do the numbers mean on grandma's headstone?"

"Well son," the grandpa replied. "The first number represents the day you are born, and the last number represents the day you pass, and do you see that little line in between them?"

"Yes grandpa," the boy answered. Grandpa paused to regain his composure and with a shaken voice said, "That little line in between represents your entire life."

What will that little dash represent in your life?

You are the author of your own life. You get to choose to either life a life full of regret and disappointment or a life full of joy, struggle and meaning. You do not get to blame the world for not dealing you the same cards of the lucky few.

It has been a healthy experience to think back across my life, reliving some lowlights, and appreciating the highlights. I have been incredibly blessed, but I am very thankful for the struggles.

It is during the struggles that we get to determine what kind of person we choose to be. We do not need to be held hostage by the mistakes we have made. We can forgive ourselves and those people who have hurt us.

We do not have to drag our past behind every step we take forward. What an unnecessary and mentally exhausting burden.

I made the decision a long time ago to keep my past tucked away in a sealed box. So much of it is kryptonite. It's not that I refuse to deal with it, I already have. There is no need to dwell on it when the only result would be anger and resentment resulting in me feeling sorry for myself.

So many people are held back from joy and happiness because they are victims of their own thoughts. If you are personally struggling with your past, I would encourage you to seek professional help if your past is haunting you and you are unable to deal with it on your own. There is no shame in healing yourself.

I would also recommend you spend time on your spiritual life. Every success principle ever written by any author has likely existed in the Bible for thousands of years. Read the Bible and you will discover truth that empowers.

Remember that principles never change, but practices do. Identify key principles that will help change your life and adopt those principles into your own, personal practices. I want my dash to mean something, do you?

MEDIOCRITY MASTERED

WHEN I STARTED THIS BOOK I DESCRIBED THE MOMENT when I was standing in that beautiful conference room in Beverly Hills reflecting on my journey as that little boy from the broken home living in small town America to the owner of the top gaming security integration company in North America.

We met with some amazing companies in that board room but ultimately, we decided to continue on our own journey of growth. It was a great learning experience and I left with a renewed commitment to build the most dominant gaming security company on this continent.

It's been a wild ride but all along the way we have looked at various principles that, when implemented, have the power to change the course of your life and that can enable you to be the master of mediocrity. Below are just some of the things I covered:

- Time will either promote you or expose you.
- Your success in life will be in direct proportion to the sum total of all your decisions, good or bad.
- Commit yourself to continuous learning.
- There are plenty of subject matter experts who have written classic books and host podcasts. Leverage them!

- The best experience is somebody else's. Use their life experiences to fuel your own growth.
- Seek counsel from people who are willing to help you and be humble enough to learn.
- Develop a plan for your life and allow your daily goals to guide you.
- Most importantly, dream big and never allow anyone to kill your dream.
- To live a life of purpose it is imperative you live it on purpose.
- Nothing of value happens by accident.
- It does not require much character to be average.
- Decide to do a little more every day.
- Fight against the comfort of mediocrity so you can live a life the average will never know.

I hope that everybody finds happiness and meaning. I hope that everyone can live a life full of joy and love. True happiness is not free, it comes through struggle and sacrifice. Like anything else of value, it will never happen by accident, it will only happen by design. It is imperative that you have, or create, a vision for your life.

Proverbs 29:18 KJV sums this up perfectly: "Where there is no **vision**, the people **perish**."

Do you want your head stone to say John Smith was born in 1990 and died in 2020, but he was buried in 2040?

How many people have you come across that are old and bitter, only talking about their past regrets in life?

It is because their dreams died long before they were buried, and they settled for a mediocre existence. I have also met people that are in their seventies and eighties who are still excited about life. They have more energy than a teenager who sits playing video games twenty-four hours a day!

Your life has already prepared you for success. You were built to win from the moment you took your first breath and will be until the moment you take your last. You are not held hostage because of the poor decisions your parents may have made. Choose to be different, fight to master mediocrity.

Maybe you were always the last kid to get picked to be on a team. Perhaps you had a learning disability that made you feel like the dumbest person in the room. Your parents divorced. You had an alcoholic or abusive parent. You were poor. You were the middle child. You were made fun of and the list goes on and on.

For every excuse to fail, there is a story of someone who overcame that same excuse to win. These events can either be reasons to fail or they can be reasons to succeed. You get to decide to be a victim or to be a victor.

People who choose to victimize themselves make me sick with all the negativity they spew. Unless we are very careful, they can infect our attitudes if we expose ourselves to them.

I dare you to dream big and create a vision for your future. Forget the past, expect great things, speak positive, and fight for what you want in life!

Inundate yourself with pictures of your future. Write down in detail your goals and read them morning, noon and right before you go to sleep.

Develop a plan of action and commit to forward progress. Turn off the negative media and read books that teach and promote personal growth. Surround yourself people who will encourage you while keeping you accountable.

Choose to be different. Do everything you can to prepare yourself for opportunities. Become the best employee you can be.

Make yourself irreplaceable. Be promotable and stand out from the crowd.

We may only get a few chances in life to achieve greatness so be ready, keep your head up and eyes open.

May you be the best version of you!

LOVE LETTER TO MY GRANDKIDS

MORE THAN ANYTHING I WANT ALL OF YOU TO KNOW that I love you with all my heart and soul. I will always be with you. You. As long as I can remember, what I wanted more than anything else was to have a big, loving family. My dream has come true.

My greatest assets are the memories I am making with you, my family. Someday, when I am getting ready to pass, I will be blessed thinking about all the great memories we have made together. I won't be thinking about the things I've purchased, I will be appreciating the people I love.

There is no greater priority in my life than the health and well-being of my family. When God blessed me with grandma, we committed to build a strong foundation that would stand the test of time. If I am the brick, then she is the mortar that has held us all together. Love and appreciate grandma forever, I will.

My wish for you is that you get to experience the instant love and bond when your miracle babies are born. I have made many mistakes as a parent and so will you. Love with all your heart and when you make parenting mistakes. Ask your kids for forgiveness. You will teach them a valuable lesson about love and grace.

There is nothing more important to me in this world than my family. I am incredibly proud of my children, and now their children. I love that we are all committed to getting together. Sunday family dinners are the best.

Be proud of your family name, Flowers and Mount. I have taught my kids when they leave the house, they are representing the family name and so are you. Treat it with respect and honor.

Love yourself, there is nobody else in this world like you. You are unique and special. Ignore the negative opinions of people who do not hold your best interests in their heart. There will always be people who will try to hold you back from achieving your dreams, avoid them like the plague.

Do not allow yourself to be influenced by whatever media exists during your lifetime. Media is nothing more than negative propaganda driving special interests of others who want to control your value system.

Wisdom comes from life experience, and the best experience is someone else's experience. Learn from those who have come before you. Be a thinker. Question the status quo.

Have the courage to be different. Be the best version of you. Be the leader, but when you must follow, be the best follower you can be.

Be curious. Have a teachable spirit. Surround yourself with people who challenge and encourage you, people who will hold you accountable.

Life is going to deliver you heartbreak and challenge. Expect it. But know that God has already equipped you with the tools to overcome anything. Lean into your faith, lean into your family, and know that time heals.

Be careful what you spend your time thinking about. You are the author of your own thoughts. Understand that just because you are thinking it, that does not make it real. Learn to recognize your moods, and avoid critical discussions and decision making when you are in a down mood. Recognize when your loved ones are in a down mood and give them the grace to work through it before you address any challenges.

Managing finances and raising kids is difficult for every couple. You can avoid many heated discussions by addressing those topics when you are both in a healthy state of mind.

Dream big. Dream your own dreams. Write your own music, live life to your own beat. Spend your life in pursuit of what brings you joy and happiness instead of trying to meet the expectations and limitations other people want to place on you. People will try to keep you down in a place of mediocrity, it makes them feel better about their own unwillingness to grow.

Value hard work, nothing of value comes easy. Manage your money!! Learn to live below your means and pay yourself first. Read the book *The Richest Man in Babylon*. It is a wonderful parable that will teach you basic financial principles. Avoid financing things just to look good or impress other people. It isn't the hood ornament on your car that will impress other people, it'll be your character.

Embrace humility and give to others. Remember that status is a nasty disease that makes everyone feel sickened, except for the person who has it.

Harness the power of compounding. If you are paying compounding interest on debt, you are losing. If you are earning compounding interest on investments, you are winning. All the little things you do, every day, will either make you or break you. This includes your thoughts and your actions. The compound effect of your thoughts and actions over time will either promote you or expose you. Time does not care about your feelings, she is the purest of multipliers compounding the sum of your actions into results, positive or negative. There is no neutral.

You will make mistakes. Learn from them and never allow your mistakes to hold you hostage. If you wrong someone, especially your wife, husband, son, or daughter, immediately ask for forgiveness. If somebody wrongs you, even if they do not ask you, give them grace and forgiveness so you are not held hostage by their mistakes.

Try not to measure other people's weaknesses against your strengths. If you do, they will never measure up to your expectations, and remember, your family are people too.

Be good humans. Invest time and money into your own personal growth. I encourage you to continue to grow as a person throughout your whole life. Find a way to give back to the world from which you take. Do your best to uplift and inspire other people. See people for who they can be not who they are, especially the person looking back at you in the mirror.

Have fun and laugh. You can work hard and have fun doing it.

Be willing to take some risks in life in pursuit of your dreams. There is nothing sadder to see than someone who is living a life full of regrets.

Love with your whole heart.

Embrace your imperfections. Those are the things that make you unique and beautiful. Do not change yourself in attempt to meet the plastic expectations of society.

Stay a kid for as long as you can. Protect your innocence and do not give it away easily or let anyone take it from you. You will experience relationships that will cause heartache, especially in the early years of your life. But it is worth the risk.

Don't rush into marriage, but when you do make the decision to marry the person of your dreams, be sure the person is someone who inspires you to grow, and become a better person, not someone who drags you down. It is not your job to spend the rest of your life trying to fix them.

Girls find your own way in life. Make your own money. Buy your own house. Do not rely on any man to come along and pay for your lifestyle. Create it all by yourself. Then, when the right man does come along, who meets your tough standards, together you can conquer the world.

Guys treat all women with respect. Women are God's gift to humanity and are the glue that holds the world together and always remember, that girl is someone's daughter! Boys understand that women are complex beings and you may never fully understand them, but do your best just to listen.

Girls, please realize that us guys are stupid and no matter how hard you try, we are probably not going to get it. Give us grace and know that we will die for you when you believe in us.

Invest in your spiritual life. Seek the answers that fill your heart with love and purpose. All the answers you will ever need to live a life that is full of love, joy and meaning can be found through spiritual growth.

You have been put on this earth to do great things. The beautiful news is that you are in complete control of the type of life you get to live. You are not a victim just because life gets hard, and it will.

My prayer for you is that all of you find your true purpose in life. Live life on purpose with purpose. It will not happen by accident.

Love you for eternity,
Papa

CPSIA information can be obtained
at www.ICGtesting.com
Printed in the USA
FSHW020832160920
73574FS